D1085030

Tina Fey
Queen of Comedy

By Melissa Raé Shofner

Portions of this book originally appeared in
Tina Fey by Lauri S. Friedman.

LUCENT
PRESS

Published in 2017 by
Lucent Press, an Imprint of Greenhaven Publishing, LLC
353 3rd Avenue
Suite 255
New York, NY 10010

Copyright © 2017 Greenhaven Press, a part of Gale, Cengage Learning
Gale and Greenhaven Press are registered trademarks used herein under
license.

All new materials copyright © 2017 Lucent Press, an Imprint of
Greenhaven Publishing, LLC.

All rights reserved. No part of this book may be reproduced in any form
without permission in writing from the publisher, except by a reviewer.

Designer: Deanna Paternostro
Editor: Vanessa Oswald

Cataloging-in-Publication Data

Names: Shofner, Melissa Raé.
Title: Tina Fey: queen of comedy / Melissa Raé Shofner.
Description: New York : Lucent Press, 2017. | Series: People in the news|
Includes index.
Identifiers: ISBN 9781534560338 (library bound) | ISBN 9781534560345
(ebook)
Subjects: LCSH: Fey, Tina, 1970---Juvenile literature. | Television actors
and actresses--United States--Biography--Juvenile literature. | Women
television writers--United States--Biography--Juvenile literature. |
Women comedians--United States--Biography--Juvenile literature.
Classification: LCC PN2287.F4255 S46 2017 | DDC 791.4502'8092--dc23

Printed in the United States of America

CPSIA compliance information: Batch #CW17KL: For further information contact Greenhaven Publishing LLC,
New York, New York at 1-844-317-7404.

Please visit our website, www.greenhavenpublishing.com. For a free
color catalog of all our high-quality books, call toll free 1-844-317-7404
or fax 1-844-317-7405.

Contents

Foreword

We live in a world where the latest news is always available and where it seems we have unlimited access to the lives of the people in the news. Entire television networks are devoted to news about politics, sports, and entertainment. Social media has allowed people to have an unprecedented level of interaction with celebrities. We have more information at our fingertips than ever before. However, how much do we really know about the people we see on television news programs, social media feeds, and magazine covers?

Despite the constant stream of news, the full stories behind the lives of some of the world's most newsworthy men and women are often unknown. Who was Taylor Swift before she was a pop music phenomenon? What does LeBron James do when he is not playing basketball? What inspired Elon Musk to dream as big as he does?

This series aims to answer questions like these about some of the biggest names in pop culture, sports, politics, and technology. While the subjects of this series come from all walks of life and areas of expertise, they share a common magnetism that has made them all captivating figures in the public eye. They have shaped the world in some unique way, and—in many cases—they are poised to continue to shape the world for many years to come.

These biographies are not just a collection of basic facts. They tell compelling stories that show how each figure grew to become a powerful public personality. Each book aims to paint a complete, realistic picture of its subject—from the challenges they overcame to the controversies they caused. In doing so, each book reinforces the idea that even the most famous faces on the news are real people who are much more complex than we are often shown in brief video clips or sound bites. Readers are also reminded that there is even more to a person than what they present to the world through social media posts, press releases, and interviews. The whole story of a person's life can only be discovered by digging beneath the surface of their public persona, and that is what this series allows readers to do.

The books in this series are filled with enlightening quotes from speeches and interviews given by the subjects, as well as quotes and anecdotes from those who know their story best: family, friends, coaches, and colleagues. All quotes are noted to provide guidance for further research. Detailed lists of additional resources are also included, as are timelines, indexes, and unique photographs. These text features come together to enhance the reading experience and encourage readers to dive deeper into the stories of these influential men and women.

Fame can be fleeting, but the subjects featured in this series have real staying power. They have fundamentally impacted their respective fields and have achieved great success through hard work and true talent. They are men and women defined by their accomplishments, and they are often seen as role models for the next generation. They have left their mark on the world in a major way, and their stories are meant to inspire readers to leave their mark, too.

A Newsworthy Comedian

Tina Fey is a bright star who stands out in the world of female comedians. She is a smart, witty woman who can seemingly do it all. Fey writes, acts, directs, produces, and even casts her own comedic productions. Her fresh ideas are both funny and thought-provoking, and her humor is sharp but remarkably "clean." Through her humor, Fey provides searing and undeniably feminist social commentary that is uniquely her own.

Fey's career in comedy started behind the scenes as a writer, but she stepped into the spotlight on television shows such as *30 Rock* and in films such as *Mean Girls*. Then, in 2008, she gained national attention when she impersonated Alaska governor Sarah Palin, the Republican nominee for vice president of the United States. Fey's Palin was an instant, headline-making hit. She was spot-on in her impressions of the governor, and America went wild. It was not long before "Tina Fey" was a household name across the country.

Being Governor "Feylin"

Fey first appeared as Palin on *Saturday Night Live* (*SNL*), a long-running sketch comedy TV show, in the fall of 2008. In one

SNL sketch, she appeared with her friend, comedian Amy Poehler, who played Democratic presidential hopeful Hillary Clinton, and delivered the famous line: "I can see Russia from my house." In another, Fey parodied a series of disastrous interviews that the real Palin had given CBS reporter Katie Couric. Fey also played Palin in a mock vice-presidential debate and in a satirical scene that took place in the White House's Oval Office. In each of these performances, Fey's mastery of Palin's looks, speech patterns, and mannerisms—not to mention the clever satirical dialogue written mostly by Fey herself—enchanted the public. "Beyond all reasonable doubt, Sarah Fey and Tina Palin are one,"[1] observed one international reporter.

Tina Fey's career in comedy has allowed her to enjoy many unique opportunities.

Immediately, the wildly popular performances crossed over from the headlines of entertainment magazines and were featured in articles in heavy-hitting news sources, such as the *New York Times* and *Los Angeles Times*, and on political websites such as Salon.com and *Huffington Post*. As a result, Fey was named one of America's 10 most fascinating people by legendary journalist Barbara Walters and as one of the most influential people of the year by *TIME* magazine. Her impressions of the Republican vice-presidential candidate were credited with shaping the national dialogue about the election and even influencing Americans' votes. A poll conducted by the *Washington Times*, for example, found that a "Tina Fey effect" was turning voters off to both Palin and her running mate, John McCain. When the two eventually lost the election, many wondered if Fey's performances had played a part in the outcome.

Accidental Politics

The fact that the *SNL* sketches were considered to be politically relevant surprised Fey. The comedian had intended to make a splash, but she had never dreamed she would have any hand in influencing the outcome of an election. The fervor over her appearances on *SNL* during the election season overwhelmed her at times, and she was not entirely comfortable with her new position as the nation's political mouthpiece. She also did not like that people interpreted her comedy bits as her political opinion.

For example, she performed a piece on *SNL*'s "Weekend Update" segment in which she defended Hillary Clinton, who at the time was running against Barack Obama to be the Democratic presidential nominee. The election was exciting because never before had a woman and an African American battled for a presidential nomination. After Fey's performance, the country seized on the comments she made during the segment, using them to champion the idea of a female presidential candidate. However, Fey had done the segment as a joke—she had not intended the nation to take the bit so seriously. Also, Fey was perceived as being Clinton's number-one fan, a title she was uncomfortable with because she was not necessarily a Clinton supporter.

Fey has received praise for her impersonation of Sarah Palin. Shown here is the costume she wore as Palin in an *SNL* skit with Amy Poehler in 2008.

While Fey immensely enjoyed playing Palin, she was surprised that people took her performances to mean that she disliked the Alaska governor. She claimed to hold real respect for Palin, saying, "That lady is a media star. She is a fascinating person. She's very likable. She's fun to play."[2] Fey approached the impressions of the governor as pure comedy and never intended for Americans to infer that she was trying to influence the outcome of the election with any of her performances.

A Modest Role Model

In the fury that led up to the election, Fey's sketches seemed to take on a life of their own. Her performances showed the extent to which entertainment can influence the most important issues of the day. Interestingly, even without the Palin sketches, Fey had already developed a large following through her realistic

Fey is shown here at an event at the famous Radio City Music Hall in 2007.

and varied portrayals of women. Fey has tackled the subjects of infertility and sexism and, through her characters, has portrayed the hardships of being a single, professional woman who has to contend with tough, male-centric environments. Because of her impressive body of work, it seems that "Tina really is the new woman who can have it all," as Donna Langley of Universal Pictures once said. "She's crossed all these barriers and milestones as a woman, so it makes her a great role model."[3]

What also makes Fey a great role model is that she does not see herself as one. In fact, she remains a modest woman known as a hard worker who wants to spend time with her family and tackle interesting, unique projects that will make people laugh and think. Fey has risen to the top of the comedy world, relying on her sharp wit and writing skills, all the while staying true to herself.

A Funny Upbringing

Elizabeth Stamatina Fey was born on May 18, 1970. "Tina," as she came to be called, grew up in the Greek and Italian neighborhood of Upper Darby, a suburb of Philadelphia, Pennsylvania. She was not the first person in her family to go by another name. Fey's mother, who is Greek, goes by "Jeanne," even though her real name is Zenobia. Fey's father, Donald, who passed away in 2015, was German and Scottish.

Fey's parents had a good sense of humor, and she got along well with them. Her father worked mainly as a grant writer for the University of Pennsylvania. In his spare time, he wrote mystery novels and served as a paramedic. Fey admired her father's wide range of skills, as well as his dedication to pursuing his interests. Her mother was a sharp-witted homemaker whom she greatly respected. Each week, her mother and her mother's friends would play poker. Fey remembers these times fondly. "I loved hanging out with the ladies because they were very funny, and a little bit mean, and had lots of Entenmann's products [a brand of baked goods],"[4] Fey said.

Fey's only sibling is her brother, Peter. He is eight years older, but they got along well growing up. Fey has said the gap in age between them made it feel as though she grew up with three parents. Still, she considers Peter to be one of her first comedic influences. He would often reenact sketches from *SNL* that inspired Fey and would later help launch her career. Fey's mother embraced her own lively sense of humor, performing comedy routines for her children at the dinner table.

Fey's vivid and sometimes strange imagination was evident from an early age through her writing and artwork. A sketch she drew when she was around seven years old showed people walking down the street holding hands. The people carried large

Tina Fey is shown here with her mother. Family has always been important to her.

pieces of Camembert, Swiss, and cheddar cheeses. The sketch was captioned "What a friend we have in cheeses!"[5] Young Fey was also known for her sharp one-liners. According to her brother, Fey had a very intelligent type of humor. "She would zing you, and a few seconds later you'd react. Like, 'Did a 14-year-old just say that?'"[6]

Fey recalls watching a lot of television when she was young. She probably watched more than the average child of her generation, but her parents likely did not mind because they loved watching comedy shows, too. "My parents mainly wouldn't let me watch stuff that was either annoying to them, or just garbage," she remembers. "My dad wouldn't let us watch *The Flintstones* if he was home because he said it was a rip-off of *The Honeymooners*."[7] Fey's career was likely influenced by the popular television shows she watched during her childhood. Her favorites were comedies such as *Laverne & Shirley*, *The Mary Tyler Moore Show*, *The Love Boat*, and *Newhart*. Fey recalls that her parents would let her watch *SNL* with them. They also loved Marx Brothers movies and once snuck Fey into a movie theater to see Mel Brooks's *Young Frankenstein*.

A Mysterious Attack

Though Tina's childhood was overwhelmingly defined by happiness and laughter, she suffered a terribly traumatic event that would haunt her well into adulthood. When she was five years old, a stranger ran up to her as she was playing in the front yard of her house. The person cut her on the left side of her face with a knife. At first, Tina thought someone had marked her with a pen. However, when blood started flowing, she knew it was something much worse. She was slashed from the corner of her mouth up several inches alongside her cheek. The incident left Fey with both physical and emotional scars, and the police never were able to identify her attacker.

Fey rarely discusses the scar, which has resulted in a lot of mystery. For years, reporters speculated about its cause, and a

The scar Fey received from her childhood attacker can be seen in this photo of her that was taken on the red carpet at the 2016 Academy Awards.

whole website called Tina Fey Scar Detective was devoted to figuring out what had happened to her. Finally, Fey discussed it publicly in a 2009 interview published in *Vanity Fair*, saying only that as a child, she did not feel any less attractive because of the scar: "I proceeded unaware of it. I was a very confident little kid.

It's really almost like I'm kind of able to forget about it, until I was on-camera, and it became a thing." As for why she does not discuss it in more detail or more often, Fey just said, "It's impossible to talk about it without somehow seemingly exploiting it and glorifying it."[8] Fey also discussed the incident in her 2011 book *Bossypants*.

Though Fey has commented minimally on the attack, others close to her have speculated on how they think it has affected both her personality and her work. "I think it really informs the way she thinks about her life," said her husband, Jeff Richmond. "When you have that kind of thing happen to you, that makes you scared of certain things, that makes you frightened of different things, your comedy comes out in a different kind of way, and it also makes you feel for people."[9] In his opinion, Fey's penchant for humor might spring from her desire to find the humor in even the darkest and saddest experiences.

Another person who has talked with Fey about the experience is Marci Klein, an executive producer of Fey's show, *30 Rock*, and the daughter of fashion designer Calvin Klein. When she was 11 years old, Klein was kidnapped for a day, and Fey felt a kinship over their shared traumas. After hearing of Klein's experience, Fey reportedly reached out to her, saying, "Well, you know, Marci, we had the Bad Thing happen to us. We know what it's like."[10]

Though Tina herself is often tight-lipped about the slashing incident, she alluded to it in the writing she has done for *30 Rock*. Her character, Liz Lemon, is much like Fey—sarcastic and even a little mean at times. After hearing one of her famously sharp quips, her boss tells her, "I don't know what happened in your life that caused you to develop a sense of humor as a coping mechanism. Maybe it was some sort of brace or corrective boot you wore during childhood, but in any case I'm glad you're on my team."[11] It is possible that in writing these lines, Fey was trying to tell the world a little about the early experience that shaped her personality so significantly. Many have also stated that allusions to Fey's childhood trauma can be found in her television show *Unbreakable Kimmy Schmidt*, which is about a woman who was kidnapped as a girl.

Fighting Insecurity

After recovering from the slashing incident, Tina attended Cardington-Stonehurst Elementary School and Beverly Hills Middle School, both in Upper Darby. As early as fifth grade, she was relying on humor as a way to make friends. "I figured out that I could ingratiate myself to people by making them laugh. Essentially, I was just trying to make them like me," she said. "But after a while it became part of my identity."[12] She also used humor as a distraction and defense mechanism. In eighth grade, she wrote a note to her math teacher that apologized for making jokes so often in class, and she admitted it was because she struggled with the subject.

As a student at Upper Darby High School, Fey continued to exhibit clear signs of the intelligent, yet also biting, personality that has defined her career. Fey remembers being mean in high school—not because she was a nasty or cruel person, but because she felt intimidated by her classmates and envied some of them. "Technically, I was a jealous girl," she said. "But because I was jealous, I was mean."[13] She made friends with a group of smart, nerdy students who all took advanced placement (AP) classes. From a safe distance in the lunchroom, they made up biting nicknames for their peers who were prettier or more athletic than them. For example, she and her friends called the preppy, pretty, popular girls the "Laura Ashley Parade" after the designer, and they called the long-haired drinkers in the partying crowd the "Hammers" because of the physical stunts they pulled at parties.

Fey remembers giving a crude nickname to the prettiest girl in her school because she was jealous. "I know [I] was really scraping the bottom of the barrel, insult-wise," she said. "But I was super-jealous of her, and dealt with it by being sarcastic behind her back."[14] Interestingly, Fey's mean streak was moralistic, and she directed the worst of her ridicule at students who drank or took drugs, ditched classes, dressed inappropriately for school, or were promiscuous.

Perhaps it was her intelligence that made Fey feel like she could

A Star-Studded
Acting Troupe

The Second City acting troupe was an important part of Tina Fey's early career. The troupe was first formed in the 1950s by students at the University of Chicago. The group puts on shows, or revues, that feature a mix of improvised and scripted sketches. Each revue also features a second act in which actors perform completely improvised scenes that are based on suggestions and ideas from audience members.

Second City has launched the careers of many notable actors. Jeremy Piven (*Entourage*) was with the group in 1988, as was Mike Myers (*Wayne's World, Austin Powers, Shrek*). Steve Carell, of *The Office* and *Crazy, Stupid, Love*, joined the group in 1991. Stephen Colbert, of *The Late Show with Stephen Colbert* and *The Colbert Report*, was with the group in 1993 and was originally hired to be Carell's understudy. Though not all Second City alumni go on to enjoy such luminous careers, the group is considered to be a hotbed of creativity and a pool of serious talent for network producers to pull from when they cast television shows and movies.

Stephen Colbert and Steve Carell are shown here on the set of *The Late Show with Stephen Colbert* in 2015. Colbert and Carell were both members of Second City.

Improv Theater

Tina Fey knows how to make things up as she goes along thanks to one specific kind of comedy training. Known as "improv," improvisational theater uses specific techniques to create spontaneous, unrehearsed performances. Many improv troupes take suggestions from the audience to create a setting and plot for the sketch. To be successful at improv, one must be a good listener, have extreme confidence, and possess instinctual performing skills.

Improv theater is believed to date back to Europe in the 1500s. Street performers used improv techniques to entertain crowds and earn money. It became a more formalized technique in the late 1800s, when directors began using improv to train and rehearse actors. In the 20th century, improv games became heavily featured in high school theater classrooms and as a part of corporate training programs to encourage employees to open up and build trust with one another.

Viola Spolin, one of the creators of modern improv, trained the first generation of improv actors in troupes, such as the Compass Players and Second City. The

technique has been worked into films, such as *This Is Spinal Tap*, and television shows, such as *Curb Your Enthusiasm*.

Second City, shown here, is known for its use of improv.

make fun of other people; perhaps it was a lack of confidence she had in her own abilities. In fact, it is possible that Fey made fun of pretty girls because she herself felt insecure about her looks. "I had a pretty rough puberty," she remembers. "Growing up as a girl is always traumatizing, especially when you have the deadly combination of greasy skin and [a body that changed earlier than most]."[15] Either way, her knack for satirizing her classmates would evolve into a career in comedy. Her own experiences in high school later informed her work on *Mean Girls*, a movie about how vicious high school girls can be to one another. As an adult, Fey realizes she was mean to others because she and her friends were insecure about themselves. "We thought we were super cool, but we were our own sad little clique,"[16] she once admitted.

It Started with the Colonel

Despite her mean streak, Fey was considered a good kid. She was an honors student who took mostly high-level AP classes. Looking back, she compares herself to Lisa Simpson from *The Simpsons* television show—a smart, know-it-all type who never drank, did drugs, had sex, or got into any trouble. She rarely had boyfriends, and when she did, they were always nice boys who never got away with much. "I was so obedient," she said, "someone should do a study of my parents and find out whatever it was they did."[17] Since she always finished her work quickly, she had a lot of time to load up her schedule with extracurricular activities. She was a staff member of the *Oak*, the school's yearbook. She also sang with the group the Encore Singers and performed in many school musicals and plays.

Her major high school pastime, though, was writing. She was editor for the school's newspaper, the *Acorn*, and in that position, wrote a regular satire column. She did not use her real name, but wrote her columns under the pseudonym "the Colonel." Using a pseudonym made Fey feel safe to deliver scathing criticisms of her school environment, and she frequently wrote about school policy and teachers. Sometimes, she got in trouble for her biting

Fey grew up in Upper Darby, Pennsylvania, shown here.

comments—Fey remembers that one time, "I got busted because I was trying to say that something would 'go down in the annals of history,' but it was a double-entendre … and I didn't get away with it."[18]

Writing as "the Colonel" was one of the activities that convinced Fey she wanted to go into comedy. She said she knew she wanted to be a comedian starting in the eighth

Using a Pseudonym

A pseudonym (also called a pen name) is a fake name used by a writer to disguise his or her identity. Like Tina Fey, many well-known writers have used a pen name at some point in their career. One of the most famous pseudonyms is "Mark Twain," which was the pen name of writer Samuel Clemens.

Writers have various reasons for using a pen name. In the days when it was frowned upon for women to write distinguished works of literature, female authors would use male pen names to get their work published. A well-known example is the writer Mary Ann Evans, who wrote under the name George Eliot. Other female authors who used pen names include Jane Austen and the Brontë sisters. Other writers may want to distinguish their literary writing from other work. This was the reasoning behind mathematician Charles Dodgson's decision to write fiction under the name Lewis Carroll. Today, writers use pen names to protect their identity (for example, if they are writing sensitive political material) or to see whether audiences will still like their work, even if unconnected to their name. This is the reason why author Stephen King has published several novels under the name Richard Bachman.

grade, when, as a reward for finishing her classroom work early, she and another student were allowed to do an independent study project on a topic of their choosing. "She chose to do hers on communism, and I chose to do mine on comedy,"[19] Fey said. Fey's high school experiences with mockery, writing, and theater groomed her well for her future in improvisational satirical comedy. She left high school on the defensive, cynical note that defined her time there, writing in the yearbook that in 10 years she was likely to be "very,

very, fat." She explained: "I was just trying to cover my bases. If I did turn out to be a pudgy loser, I'd be able to say, 'See, I told you.'"[20]

Fey Goes to College

After graduating from high school in 1988, Fey moved to Charlottesville, Virginia, to attend the University of Virginia. Charlottesville was a totally new and different environment for the Pennsylvania native. Fey was enamored with the distinctly southern, genteel atmosphere—and the overwhelming number of blondes she encountered everywhere. She originally majored in English because of her natural interest in and talent for writing. However, she quickly left the department, claiming it was too snobbish for her taste. She switched her major to her second love—drama—and promptly became a self-described theater nerd.

Fey attended the University of Virginia in Charlottesville from 1988 until 1992.

Fey recalls dressing outside the mainstream, favoring black tights, Doc Martens, and baby-doll dresses. As a college student, she continued to nurture her sarcastic mean streak, making fun of the typical university types around her. She also maintained her values: Although she went to parties where there was drinking, she never drank. She also preferred to live on campus for longer than most students, reportedly to be close to the university's theater.

It was during her years in Virginia that she started to write scripts and comedy bits, learning skills that would provide the foundation of her career. She also performed in several theatrical productions, holding notable roles. As a senior, she played Sally Bowles, the lead role in the musical *Cabaret*. She frequently performed a monologue from a Tennessee Williams play called *This Property Is Condemned*. Unlike many college students who spent their summers working odd jobs or traveling, Fey spent the months off involved with Summer Stage theater productions. She sang and acted in some performances and spent two summers as a director.

Joining the Cult of Improvisation

Many students graduate from college unsure of what direction to take in life, but not Fey. After graduating from the University of Virginia in 1992, she immediately moved to Chicago, where she took classes from the illustrious improvisational comedy troupe Second City. Second City is known for churning out dozens of great comedians—and many future *SNL* alumni, including Bill Murray, Mike Myers, Chris Farley, Tim Meadows, Rachel Dratch, and Amy Poehler. In fact, the whole reason Fey was interested in Second City was because, as she explained, "I knew it was where a lot of *SNL* people had started."[21] Through the group, Fey took improv classes and acting workshops. While she honed her craft, she supported herself with a job in child care at the local YMCA. In order to keep her evenings free to take improv classes, she worked the 5:30 a.m. to 2:00 p.m. shift at the YMCA.

In 1994, after two years in training, she was invited to join the group as an understudy in their touring ensemble. She toured for a little less than a year and eventually began performing on their main stage. In this position, she wrote and performed monologues, sketches, and one-act plays. She held this position for about a year and a half. As a Second City performer, Fey stood out not just for being funny, but also for being a funny female. Jeff Richmond, her husband, recalled, "I don't want to say she was funny 'for a woman,' but there were so many talented men there at the time, and then suddenly there was Tina, who was so funny—and she was at home with all those boys on the stage."[22]

Fey and her husband, Jeff Richmond, met while they were part of Second City. The two have been working on film and television projects together ever since.

Learning the craft of improvisation helped acting make sense to Fey. She described it as helping her body and emotions become free enough to truly channel a character, rather than just imitate one. Furthermore, the go-with-the-flow aspect of improv appealed to Fey and helped guide her in her offstage life. "I've found the general philosophy of it to be quite helpful," she said. "It reminds me that if I stumble onto something unexpected in my writing, something that I didn't anticipate or intend, I should be willing to follow it."[23]

By 1997, it seemed that Fey was well on her way to accomplishing everything she had set out to do. For starters, she was performing improv comedy on a nightly basis with one of the most renowned comedy troupes in the country. She had also met her future husband, a level-headed midwesterner who shared her values—and, as a piano player for Second City, also shared her love for the improvisational arts. Although Fey had been drawn to Second City as a route to *SNL*, she quickly came to love the improvisational life for its own merits. "I became immersed in the cult of improvisation," she said. "I was so sure that I was doing exactly what I'd been put on this earth to do, and I would have done anything to make it onto that stage. Not because of *SNL*, but because I wanted to devote my life to improv."[24] She said that she would have been perfectly content to stay at Second City for the rest of her life, turning into an old woman there. However, Fey was about to make a bold move that would change her life forever, taking her career to heights she had never dreamed possible.

Chapter Two

Tina Fey Takes New York

At 27 years old, Tina Fey felt as if she was on top of the world. Little did she know, her life was about to get even better. Fey's friend Adam McKay had been urging her to send some sample scripts to Lorne Michaels, the executive producer of *SNL*. Fey knew McKay from his work with Second City. McKay had gone on to become the head writer at *SNL*, which is how he knew that Fey's style would be perfect for the show. In June 1997, Fey made the decision to send in some of her work. Michaels loved her writing, and just a few months later, he offered her the opportunity to be a staff writer for *SNL*.

Even though she had been interested in doing sketch comedy her whole life, Fey hesitated before taking the job with *SNL*. With Second City, she was able to write and perform live comedy in a small, intimate setting seven days a week. She was not sure if she wanted to give that up, especially since she had fallen in love with Jeff Richmond, Second City's piano player. Fey also loved Chicago and did not want to lose the feeling of being at home. However, after talking to friend Amy Poehler about the *SNL* writing gig and the money it offered, she decided not to let the opportunity slip by.

Taking the job at *SNL* was the right decision for Fey. She fit in well with the other writers and enjoyed the quirky backstage atmosphere. The noisy, crowded writers' room was intense but upbeat and filled with some of the most talented writers

Adam McKay encouraged Fey to send sample scripts to the executive producer of *SNL*.

and actors of the day. Fey was often greeted with imaginative pranks and wild antics. She and the other writers were constantly bouncing ideas for jokes and sketches off each other. "Most of the time, you're too busy to think about it, but every now and then you say, 'I work at *Saturday Night Live*,' and that is so cool,"[25] she said. Perhaps the best part of the transition to her new job in a new city was that Fey was able to save her long-distance relationship with Richmond. The two became much

The Influential Executive:
Lorne Michaels

Lorne Michaels is the charismatic and highly respected creator and producer of *SNL*. Michaels has mentored the many *SNL* comedians who have gone on to

make their own movies, including Adam Sandler, Rob Schneider, and Mike Myers. As a result, many characters in their films have been based loosely on him. The most famous of these is Dr. Evil in the *Austin Powers* series. The inflection of Dr. Evil's voice, his speech patterns, and his cool and aloof deliveries are direct reflections of Michaels's personality. Other movies and television shows that have featured characters based in part on Michaels include *Scrooged*, *Brain Candy*, and Fey's *30 Rock*.

Except for a brief period in the early 1980s, Lorne Michaels has been working with *SNL* since he created the show with Dick Ebersol in 1975.

closer when he moved to New York a few years later to compose music for *SNL* skits.

The Writing Life

Fey found life at *SNL* invigorating but also challenging. The show's weekly schedule was grueling—writers only had days to come up with funny bits, and these had to go over well with numerous people before they were ever shown to an audience. Fey remembers that for her first show, she wrote a sketch about then president Bill Clinton that did not get any laughs from the other writers when it was previewed. "This weight of embarrassment came over me, and I felt like I was sweating from my spine out," she said. "But I realized, 'OK, that happened, and I did not die.'"[26] From that experience, she learned it is important to experience failure, understand why one failed, and then move past it.

In 1999, after just two years as a staff writer, Fey was promoted to head writer—the first female head writer in *SNL* history. In this coveted position, Fey was responsible for writing two sketches a week and heading up a "rewrite table," where other writers had to preview their sketches for criticism. She was known for being fair but tough in this role, and Michaels appreciated her ability to know when to let go of an idea that had become stale or cold. As a result, Fey commanded the attention and respect of the other writers and performers. Former *SNL* cast member Jimmy Fallon said other cast members deferred to her in terms of which sketches to drop and which to pursue. "If she laughs, everyone's laughing,"[27] Fallon said.

Fey also landed a spot in a select group of writers who ultimately decided which sketches would air, which put her in the position to determine the direction of each show's content. In addition, she was given the ability to hire and fire other writers. She used her power to add more funny females to the cast. In fact, women such as Amy Poehler, Rachel Dratch, and Maya Rudolph all landed their spots on *SNL* in part because of Fey (who knew Poehler and Dratch from her time in Chicago).

Fey's dramatic—and fast—success on the show led some to complain that Michaels was playing favorites with her. However, the truth was that Michaels saw immense talent in

Michaels promoted Fey to head writer at *SNL* in 1999.

Fey and was proud to showcase it. "There's a group of people who feel Tina can do no wrong in my eyes. But that's because she's just wrong less often than other people,"[28] Michaels said.

"Weekend Update"
Leads the Way

The "Weekend Update" segment first aired on October 11, 1975, on the first *SNL* broadcast. Originally, it was anchored by Chevy Chase, who famously closed the broadcast with his signature statement, "Good night, and have a pleasant tomorrow." "Weekend Update" is *SNL*'s longest-running sketch and is often credited with launching the now-popular satirical news format. Indeed, since "Weekend Update" first aired, comedic news shows, such as *The Daily Show with Trevor Noah*, *Last Week Tonight with John Oliver*, and *Full Frontal with Samantha Bee*, have become increasingly popular.

Notable "Weekend Update" anchors have included Chase, Dennis Miller, Kevin Nealon, Norm Macdonald, Jimmy Fallon, Tina Fey (who, as anchor, brought back Chase's famous closing quip in her sign-off statements), Amy Poehler, and Seth Meyers. Many have had successful careers after leaving the "Update" desk.

Fey and Poehler served together as *SNL*'s "Weekend Update" hosts from 2004 to 2006.

An Equal-Opportunity Comedian

As head writer, Fey penned interesting, funny sketches that boosted the ratings of *SNL*. She also brought a feminist dynamic to an entertainment institution that had a die-hard reputation for being an "old boys' club." Indeed, at the time, most of the show's superstars over its two decades of existence had been men, and the majority of the writers were male, too. Women who tried to insert themselves into this atmosphere found it a difficult place to work. For example, comedian Janeane Garofalo, who spent just a few months on the show in the mid-1990s, famously criticized the male-dominated environment in *Live from New York: An Uncensored History of Saturday Night Live*, which is an official history of the show. Garofalo said she disliked the working environment so much that she wanted to quit after her first week. However, when Fey took over, Garofalo became aware of the changes. "With the Tina Fey regime, things started turning around," she said. "I think the prevailing attitude had been that women just aren't quite as funny."[29]

Janeane Garofalo was not a fan of the male-dominated atmosphere of *SNL* in the mid-1990s.

Fey was able to insert certain kinds of humor into sketches in a way that the show's male writers were uncomfortable doing. For example, she wrote jokes about feminine hygiene products, infertility, sexual abuse, and plastic surgery. Fey remembers a time when a male staff member asked if she thought her sketches were "anti-woman." Fey said it was her job to make fun of people, and including women made her an equal-opportunity comedian.

Fey is a self-proclaimed feminist, but she considers women fair game if a joke made about them is truthful. "You can't be afraid to write comedy about women because then you're just going to perpetuate the idea that women aren't as big a part of society [as men are]," she said. The trick, in Fey's eyes, is to write about women as she sees them. For example, "I'm not going to write a sketch where Hillary Clinton is a raving ... secret lesbian because that's not my perception of her," she said. "I've written things where she was the furious, put-upon wife of an adulterer, but the tone is much different because a woman is writing it."[30] Fey has stated that she feels she can make certain jokes and use certain language about women in a way that men cannot because she is a woman: "It's a little bit ... It's between us."[31]

From Writer to Co-Anchor

Fey made the transition from writer to actor after Michaels saw her perform in a comedy sketch at Upright Citizens Brigade Theatre, a popular comedy venue in New York. Michaels encouraged her to audition for the co-anchor spot on "Weekend Update," a part of each episode of *SNL* in which an anchor or anchors make light of the week's news events. Anchoring "Weekend Update" is a particularly demanding role on *SNL*. To make sure the jokes are as up-to-date as possible, writing for the segment is always done last—sometimes just hours before the show airs.

Fey cohosted "Weekend Update" with Jimmy Fallon from

Teaming Up
with Amy Poehler

Actress and comedian Amy Poehler has teamed up with Tina Fey many times. They first met in the early 1990s in Chicago, where they were both studying the art of improvisational acting. Poehler joined the cast of *SNL* in 2001, when Fey was already serving as head writer. From 2004 to 2006, the pair hosted "Weekend Update" as the first pair of women to anchor the segment. They have also made movies together. Poehler played the role of a trying-to-be-hip mother in Fey's 2004 hit *Mean Girls* and costarred with Fey in the 2008 comedy *Baby Mama*. Their most recent film together was the 2015 comedy *Sisters*.

One of Poehler and Fey's most notable team accomplishments came in 2008, when they paired up for several *SNL* sketches mocking that year's presidential campaign. In one sketch, Fey portrayed Republican vice-presidential nominee Sarah Palin while Poehler

2000 to 2004. From 2004 to 2006, she cohosted with Amy Poehler, marking the first time in *SNL*'s history that two women anchored the segment. Viewers enjoyed Fey's characteristic short, sharp barbs and smart, spirited rants into the camera.

Even though she left the show in 2006 to pursue other interests, Fey continued to make guest appearances in *SNL* sketches and on "Weekend Update." In fact, by the end of the 2008 to 2009 season, Fey had made the most appearances on "Weekend Update" of any anchor in the history of the segment. She had appeared on the program 118 times, followed by Dennis Miller (who has appeared 111 times), Poehler (81 times), and Fallon and Jane Curtin (each appeared 80 times).

depicted Democratic presidential hopeful Hillary Clinton. In another sketch, Fey played Palin while Poehler adopted the role of *CBS Evening News* interviewer Katie Couric, who did several memorable interviews with Palin in real life.

Fey and Poehler also hosted the Golden Globe Awards together in 2013, 2014, and 2015, earning rave reviews from industry insiders and fans.

Amy Poehler is a longtime friend of Tina Fey.

Total Transformation

Fey underwent a physical transformation when she came out from behind the writer's desk to star on *SNL*. At the time she was being considered for "Weekend Update," she wore bulky sweaters and reportedly favored wearing a ski cap while she wrote. She ate junk food as she worked on scripts. In short, she was not what many in the entertainment industry would call "camera-ready."

Those she worked with originally did not see her as the beautiful star she is seen as today. "When she got here, she was kind of goofy-looking,"[32] said Steve Higgins, one of the show's producers. Hollywood agent Sue Mengers remembers one night when Michaels brought Fey over to her house to see what she thought of casting Fey in "Weekend Update." "She was very mousy," remembers Mengers, who warned Michaels against putting her on camera. "She doesn't have the looks."[33]

Richmond also remembers Fey's pre–"Weekend Update" style, although with more appreciation than the others. He has said her sense of style was not particularly glamorous. She favored mismatched outfits and awkward footwear. "She would wear just a lot of knee-length ... dresses with thrift-store sweaters and kind of what was comfortable,"[34] he said.

A turning point came for Fey shortly before she auditioned for the coanchor spot on "Weekend Update." She remembers catching a glimpse of herself on a monitor around the studio, "and I was like, 'Ooogh.' I was starting to look unhealthy."[35] It was at this point that Fey started losing weight through the Weight Watchers program and dropped 30 pounds (13.6 kg). She credits Weight Watchers for her shift to a healthier lifestyle: "That's when I learned how to eat properly for the first time. Before, I used to be one of those people who wouldn't eat anything all day, then eat a piece of cake at 4 p.m., McDonald's at 10 p.m., and then go to bed."[36] Fey also makes physical activity a priority as part of a healthy lifestyle. When asked about exercise, she said, "I genuinely enjoy it. I find it very hard to fit in during the season because we work 14 to 16 hours a day, and when I get home, I want to see my family. But I prefer my life a little more if I'm exercising regularly."[37]

After Fey lost weight, she started dressing in more fashionable outfits. In a short time, she developed the look for which she is now known: sharp business suits, a smart haircut, and glasses. Fey takes a humorous approach to her image, making jokes about the ridiculous beauty standards of society. Once, when asked about her glasses during an interview, Fey responded, "You could put glasses on a rotting pumpkin, and people would think it was sexy."[38]

"Tina, Dahling, Where Have You Been?"

The change in Fey was so remarkable that people who had ignored her for years began to take notice. Said one colleague, "Steve Martin [who frequently visited the show, used to walk] right past her at the coffee table, and then, after the makeover, he was like, 'Well, hel-looo—who are you?'"[39] Alec Baldwin, her costar on *30 Rock* and a frequent host of *SNL*, has put Fey's transformation in the following way: "The collective consciousness has said, 'Tina, dahling, where have you been? Where on earth have you been?'"[40]

Soon it was not just Fey's costars who were noticing her makeover. Viewers and critics everywhere were, too. The media was quick to point out the changes as well. "I

Fey transformed her appearance into that of a major television star in the early 2000s.

think it's really funny, and I try to enjoy it," Fey said of the sudden attention. "When I was in my early twenties, being called sexy was not part of my experience in any way." Fey took the newfound interest in her appearance in stride. Ever humble and slightly self-deprecating, she said,

> There's such a small window of time when people want to write any articles about you. If you're a woman and they say anything complimentary about your appearance, well, I'm not going to complain. I fully intend to keep all of these magazines in the attic and bring them out for my daughter someday. "You see? There was a time when people thought your mother was ... sexy."[41]

Saving Saturday Night Live

Once she was behind the "Weekend Update" desk, Fey brought more than just extra laughs to *SNL*. When she joined *SNL* as a writer in 1997, the show had suffered several seasons of critically low ratings. However, Fey's work both on and off camera boosted it to heights of popularity it had not seen in nearly a decade. In 2001, the same year she was named one of *Entertainment Weekly*'s Entertainers of the Year, Fey shared a Writers Guild Award with the other *SNL* writers for her work on the show's 25th anniversary special. The following year, she helped the show win an Emmy for Outstanding Writing—an award it had not received since 1989. By 2003, *SNL* was the most popular late-night show on television, attracting more viewers than other famous programs such as *The Tonight Show with Jay Leno* and *Late Night with David Letterman*.

Fey is modest about her role in this success, saying it was the collective hard work of a talented team and that she just happened to be hired during a time when the show was on an upswing. Still, many credit Fey's snarky, sharp style with single-handedly injecting new life into *SNL* and with carving a new kind of career path for female comedians, actresses, and writers.

Chapter **Three**

Writing Her Way to Fame

Tina Fey began to tackle projects outside of *SNL* as her career took off, starting with the movie *Mean Girls*. The film, which was released in 2004, was the first of several successful endeavors that Fey pursued. The next came in 2006, when Fey decided to leave *SNL* to write and star in her own show, *30 Rock*. Following the first season of *30 Rock*, Fey starred in the movie *Baby Mama* alongside her good friend Amy Poehler. These projects reflected Fey's desire to explore women's experiences. They are also infused with the sharp, high-quality humor that she has become known for.

Teen Queens and Movie Dreams

Fey's first project outside of *SNL* was the movie *Mean Girls*, which is about the merciless world of teenage girls. The film is actually based on a nonfiction book called *Queen Bees and Wannabes: Helping Your Daughter Survive Cliques, Gossip, Boyfriends, and Other Realities of Adolescence*, which was written by by Rosalind Wiseman. The book is a sociological look at the groups teenage girls organize themselves into and was originally written as a handbook for parents. Within the book, Wiseman discusses the different social roles that girls play in high school society. In this "Girl World," Wiseman identifies several types of girls, such as popular "Queen Bee," imitator wannabes, personality-less sidekicks, information-gathering "bankers," and more.

Fey first got the idea to adapt the book into a movie after reading an article about the author in *New York Times Magazine*. The subject matter fascinated her and reminded her of her own teenage years. She saw the potential for it to be adapted into a fictional screenplay, so she took the idea to Lorne Michaels, who frequently backs the movie projects of his *SNL* actors. He liked the idea, too. Once Michaels gave it his stamp of approval, Fey called Wiseman and requested an advance copy of the book.

At first, Wiseman was reluctant. "She basically wanted me to promise her that I wouldn't take her book and make it into a cheap, dumb, dirty movie; [m]ake fun of it or sell it out,"[42] Fey said. However, after Fey reassured her that it was the smart tone of the book that interested her, Wiseman agreed to let her turn the book into a movie.

Writing from Experience

Fey had to get creative when turning the nonfiction book into a fictional movie. For material, Fey took anecdotes from the book and turned them into scenes between fictional characters. Some of the movie's most memorable scenes actually came from Fey's own teenage life. For example, she really did have a health teacher like the one portrayed by Dwayne Hill in *Mean Girls*. In the movie, his character, Coach Carr, takes a misinformed and even bullying approach to sex education. "Don't have sex because you will get pregnant and die," his character warns. "If you do touch each other, you will get chlamydia ... and die."[43] He then proceeds to hand out a bucket of condoms to the classroom of

Changing Her Ways

Mean Girls tells the story of high school girls who torment each other out of jealousy and competitiveness. Although she wrote the movie to show that this behavior is wrong, Fey herself has been accused of being mean. In high school and college, she made fun of people who were different than her. Likewise, the jokes she wrote for "Weekend Update" have been described by both audiences and colleagues as hard-edged and even cruel.

Fey recognizes she has a mean streak and has said she would like to overcome it. "I'm really trying to move away from it," she said. "Because I don't think you can have a long future in that. You can be mean and caustic in your teens and 20s, but if you keep it going, by the time you're 40, you're just going to be a [jerk]. You're just going to be an old [jerk]."[1]

1. Quoted in Emily Rems, "Mrs. Saturday Night," *Bust*, Spring 2004, p. 42.

students. Such mixed messages are famous in U.S. high schools, including Fey's own, and her spot-on depiction of them helped the movie resonate with students, parents, and teachers. Fey also based Ms. Norbury, the character she played, on another one of her real teachers from high school—her favorite German teacher.

Fey experienced a relationship similar to the one portrayed by characters Cady Heron (played by Lindsay Lohan) and Aaron Samuels (played by Jonathan Bennett), in which a girl dumbs herself down to try to get the attention of a popular, attractive boy. "[That relationship] was sort of like the fumbling, obsessive pursuit that I was trying to do in high school," Fey said. "It never worked out for me." However, Fey recognizes that she was not, in reality, very much like Cady at all. "I was somewhere in between the characters of Janice and the mathletes," she said—a little bit nerdy and filled with a distinct animosity for the prettier, more popular girls in high school. As for which of Wiseman's girl

Fey is shown here posing with Jonathan Bennett and Lindsay Lohan at the *Mean Girls* premiere after-party in 2004.

categories she best fits into, Fey said, "I was sort of a banker because I was the sort of person where, if there was gossip about someone, I wanted to know all of it in detail and have it, like, ready. The one that freely will pass on the gossip if they hear it."[44] Such girls are also portrayed in the movie.

Fey was frequently the victim of traps such as the one that character Regina George (played by Rachel McAdams) sets for Cady. In one scene, Regina tells Cady that she thinks Cady is really pretty. Instead of denying or deflecting the compliment like most insecure girls would, Cady thanks her for it. Regina takes Cady's appreciation for the compliment as a mark of arrogance. "So you agree? You think you're really pretty?"[45] Regina asks, putting Cady on the spot, seemingly accusing her of being conceited. Fey said she found herself in a similar situation once, and she resented the suggestion that liking something about herself could be a bad thing. She feels these kinds of interactions between girls discourage them from being proud of their beauty, intelligence, and talent. By adding the message to the movie, she hoped to expose the problems with such interactions and highlight how girls should work together to play up each other's best qualities, rather than cutting each other down.

A+ Reviews for Mean Girls

Fey's work schedule on *Mean Girls* was grueling. In addition to being both a writer and an actor on the project, Fey was still responsible for appearing on *SNL* in New York every weekend while the movie was being shot in Toronto. To juggle both projects at once, Fey would finish *SNL* at around 1:00 a.m. on Sunday. Then, she would take off her makeup, put on pajamas, and get directly into a motor home that shuttled her up to Canada. She would sleep the whole 8.5-hour drive and be on the set of *Mean Girls* by the morning.

Her efforts were well worth it. *Mean Girls* won acclaim from

Mean Girls was a success for both Fey and Lohan.

reviewers and moviegoers. The film was praised for providing a humorous portrayal of the real-life issues faced by teenage girls without glorifying or promoting them. As one reviewer commented, "*Mean Girls* manages to rail against stereotypes while still trafficking in them."[46] The late film critic Roger Ebert agreed, saying the movie stood out in its genre as a quality film that was as entertaining as it was thoughtful. "In a wasteland of dumb movies about teenagers," he wrote, "*Mean Girls* is a smart and funny one. It even contains some wisdom." Calling the screenplay "both a comic and a sociological achievement," Ebert concluded: "*Mean Girls* dissects high school society with a lot of observant detail, which seems surprisingly well-informed."[47]

A Show About a Show: 30 Rock

Fey had taken on the challenge of *Mean Girls* as a way of exploring what her career might look like post–*SNL*. Encouraged by the success of the movie, and emboldened by how much she enjoyed the experience, Fey left *SNL* in 2006 to pursue more projects. One of those projects was a half-hour situation comedy, or sitcom, called *30 Rock*, which was based on Fey's experiences as a writer at *SNL*.

The show was a behind-the-scenes look at the writers and actors of the fictional live variety show *The Girlie Show*. With its hastily written comedy sketches and live production in New York, *The Girlie Show* bears much resemblance to *SNL*. The main character on *30 Rock*, Liz Lemon, has a lot in common with Fey; Lemon is the head writer of the show and must constantly put up with powerful, insane, or otherwise bothersome men (and sometimes Jenna Maroney, *The Girlie Show*'s irrational and vain female lead played by Jane Krakowski). Amid their antics, Lemon struggles to keep up the quality of the show and keep its writing centered around Jenna's performances. *The Girlie Show*'s producer, played by Alec Baldwin, is based loosely on Lorne Michaels. Finally, the show's name is short for 30 Rockefeller Plaza, the

Shown here are *30 Rock* costars Jack McBrayer, Fey, Tracy Morgan, and Jane Krakowski promoting the show in New York City in 2007.

address of NBC Studios where *SNL* is filmed. In addition to being creator of the show, Fey served as head writer, executive producer, and casting director.

Upon first airing, *30 Rock* was well received by critics and reviewers, who found it smart, different, and entertaining. Despite the praise, *30 Rock* struggled to attract viewers. It initially aired Wednesday nights, which is not a high-viewing night (compared with Thursday nights, for example). Also viewers may have initially found it too similar to another NBC show, *Studio 60 on the Sunset Strip*, which was also a show-about-a-show. Although it struggled at first, *30 Rock* enjoyed greater success in its subsequent seasons.

Bringing Up Baby

Shortly after launching *30 Rock*, Fey turned her attention back to the silver screen, teaming up with former *SNL* "Weekend Update" coanchor Amy Poehler in the movie *Baby Mama*. Fey played Kate Holbrook, a successful businesswoman in her late 30s who wants to have a baby. Since she has spent so much of her life focused on her career, Kate is facing fertility issues. Desperate to have a child, she hires an obnoxious woman—Angie Ostrowski (Poehler)—to be a surrogate mother (a woman who carries another's fertilized egg to term in her womb).

Baby Mama was an original addition to the film offerings of the time for several reasons. For one, it is still rare to see a comedy that features two female leads. Many of the most popular comedies are directed by men, feature male leads, and portray events from a male perspective. As reporter Paul Brownfield put it, "It seems unusual—if not illegal—for two females … to have the leads in a buddy comedy … It's almost like an experiment in comedy science class: What if these roles went to funny women who've earned their shot at big-screen success?"[48] Secondly, *Baby Mama* covered subject matter that generally does not lend itself to humor. In fact, Fey said the subject was one of the main reasons why she was drawn to the

Baby Mama brought Fey and Poehler's friendship to the big screen for the first time.

script. "I liked the topicality of the fertility issues that affect so many people," she said. "There's so much weirdness and emotion about it. If you start with something juicy, you end up with a better [movie] than if you just start with some jokes."[49]

However, *Baby Mama* received mixed reviews from critics. "The visual style is sitcom functional, and even the zippiest jokes fall flat because of poor timing," wrote *New York Times* reviewer Manohla Dargis. "But, much like the prickly, talented Ms. Fey, [*Baby Mama*] pulls you in with a provocative and, at least in current American movies, unusual mix of female intelligence, awkwardness, and chilled-to-the-bone mean."[50] Another reviewer called it, "An essentially sweet-natured picture that doesn't go as far as it could."[51]

No matter what they thought of the movie, almost all reviewers complimented Fey and Poehler for creating a female comedy team unique to contemporary cinema. "Though the competition hasn't exactly been stiff, Fey and Poehler may well be the best female comedy duo since Lucy and Ethel,"[52] one reviewer wrote. Wesley Morris of the *Boston Globe* agreed. "In this era of [Judd] Apatow and [Will] Ferrell and [Seth] Rogen and [Owen] Wilson, of men monopolizing movie comedy, *Baby Mama* feels absurdly momentous, and even political," he wrote. "Fey and Poehler aren't just taking back control of their bodies. They're taking back control of their profession."[53]

Introducing Sarah Palin

Although both *30 Rock* and *Baby Mama* represented new steps in Fey's career, neither captured the nation's attention as much as her impression of vice-presidential candidate Sarah Palin during the 2008 election season. Republican presidential nominee John McCain took the country by surprise when he selected Palin, then the governor of Alaska, to be his running mate.

Palin was an unusual choice for the ticket. She was considered by many to be too inexperienced to fill the position of vice president. She had only served as governor for two years

Sarah Palin, shown here, burst onto the political scene in 2008.

and prior to that had been the mayor of a small Alaskan town. Because she was from Alaska, Palin also was viewed as being far outside the mainstream of U.S. politics.

Palin had a manner that polarized Americans, either for or against her. A self-described "hockey mom," she frequently delivered her political messages in folksy English. Some found this appealing and related to her "of-the-people" character. Others found her language inappropriate for a politician and questioned her intelligence. She quickly became known for making statements that dominated headlines, even if they lacked political substance. For example, she was famous for describing herself and McCain as a team of "maverick" politicians who intended to shake up U.S. politics. She also famously railed against the "liberal media," which she claimed misrepresented her words. What Palin became most famous for, however, was her long-winded and often blundering answers to questions posed by journalists and others.

"Feylin" Takes the Stage

Every presidential election season, late-night comedy shows make fun of the candidates. The 2008 election season was no exception, and Palin's nomination gave comedians unprecedented material for jokes. Her folksy, often mangled statements provided comedians with a wealth of material—and no comedian tackled Palin as well as Tina Fey. In fact, Fey returned to *SNL* to make several appearances as Palin, taking her career from red-hot to white-hot.

Fey was a natural to play Palin. The actress already resembled the governor—both had dark hair, had fair skin, and wore similar glasses. With the right wardrobe, wig, and makeup, *SNL* stylists were able to outfit Fey with Palin's trademark upswept hairdo and brightly colored, high-necked skirt suits—and the resemblance was truly remarkable.

By all accounts, Fey's impersonation was dead-on. Fey studied up on imitating Palin's twangy manner of speaking and hilariously replicated her peculiar brand of logic. In many cases, all it took for Fey to deliver a successful parody was to repeat what Palin had said during an actual interview. Before the election, Palin was interviewed several times by *CBS Evening News* anchor Katie Couric. These interviews were a gold mine for Fey. For example, when asked about America's financial problems, Palin gave Couric the following answer:

> *That's why I say, I, like every American I'm speaking with, we're ill about this position that we have been put in, where it is the taxpayers looking to bail out. But ultimately, what the bailout does is help those who are concerned about the healthcare reform that is needed to help shore up our economy, helping the—oh, it's got to be all about job creation, too, shoring up our economy and putting it back on the right track. So, healthcare reform and reducing taxes and reining in spending has got to accompany tax reductions and tax relief for Americans. And trade, we have— we've got to see trade as opportunity, not as a competitive, scary*

thing, but one in five jobs being created in the trade sector today. We've got to look at that as more opportunity. All those things under the umbrella of job creation. This bailout is a part of that.[54]

To impersonate the Alaskan governor, Fey played up Palin's stunted sentences and jumps in logic and sprinkled them with comedic elements. She kept many of the same hand gestures and facial expressions that the governor used, further giving the performance a realistic quality. Above all, Fey nailed Palin's twangy accent and folksy manner of speaking.

To get in character, Fey worked hard to adopt Palin's distinct way of talking. "She has a really crazy voice," Fey told David Letterman when she appeared on his show. "It's a little bit *Fargo*, a little bit Reese Witherspoon in *Election*. I also try and base it on my friend Paula's grandma—a sweet little ol' lady from Joliet, Illinois." To play up Palin's unique manner of speaking, Fey worked with sketch writers to use words that heavily featured the letter R. "She loves those Rs," Fey said. "I think she thinks there's oil in those Rs, she's digging deep."[55] In her rendition of the Couric interview, Fey said the following as Palin:

Like every American I'm speaking with, we're ill about this. We're saying, "Hey, why bail out Fanny and Freddie and not me?" But ultimately what the bailout does is, help those that are concerned about the healthcare reform that is needed to help shore up our economy to help … uh … it's gotta be all about job creation, too. Also, too, shoring up our economy and putting Fannie and Freddy back on the right track and so healthcare reform and reducing taxes and reining in spending … 'cause Barack Obama, y'know … we've got to accompany tax reductions and tax relief for Americans, also, having a dollar value meal at restaurants. That's gonna help. But one in five jobs being created today under the umbrella of job creation.[56]

Americans found the segment funny because Fey used so much

Sarah Palin

Sarah Palin was born in 1964 in Idaho, but her family moved to Wasilla, Alaska, when she was an infant. She spent her early years as a beauty queen, placing third in the Miss Alaska competition in 1984. Palin initially worked as a sportscaster for several Anchorage television stations and married her husband, Todd, in 1988.

She was a member of Wasilla's city council from 1992 until 1996, when she was elected the city's mayor. She served as mayor from 1996 to 2002. In 2006, she was elected the governor of Alaska—the youngest person and the first female ever to do so in that state. She did not gain national political prominence, however, until she was tapped in 2008 to be Republican presidential nominee John McCain's running mate. The pair lost the election to President Barack Obama and Vice President Joe Biden.

Palin is known for her folksy style and fiercely Christian values. She has five children. In July 2009, Palin resigned as Alaska's governor halfway through her term to pursue other endeavors.

Palin is shown here at the 2008 Republican National Convention.

of Palin's original dialogue in the parody, and thus cut to the heart of what struck Palin opponents as so ridiculous about her nomination in the first place.

"Feylin" and Foreign Policy

Palin gave Fey a lot of material over the course of the campaign. For example, when the governor was criticized for having little foreign policy experience, she argued that Alaska's nearness to Russia qualified as such. The claim was silly and exposed as hollow by most observers, including Fey, who made fun of it in a sketch later that week in which she, as Palin, said, "I can see Russia from my house!"[57] In fact, Fey's take on Palin's comment was so popular that for a while, the "I can see Russia from my house!" quote was attributed to Palin on countless blogs and forwarded e-mails.

Fey took another stab at Palin's claims to foreign policy experience by imitating another part of Palin's interview with Couric. Couric had asked Palin to further explain her foreign policy experience. The conversation went as follows:

Couric: You've cited Alaska's proximity to Russia as part of your foreign policy experience. What did you mean by that?

Palin: That Alaska has a very narrow maritime border between a foreign country, Russia, and on our other side, the land—boundary that we have with—Canada ...

Couric: Explain to me why that enhances your foreign policy credentials.

Palin: Well, it certainly does because our—our next-door neighbors are foreign countries. They're in the state that I am the executive of. And they're in Russia—

Couric: Have you ever been involved with any negotiations, for example, with the Russians?

Palin: We have trade missions back and forth. We—we do—it's very important when you consider even national security issues with Russia ... where—where do they go? It's Alaska. It's just right over the border. It is—from Alaska that we send those out to make sure that an eye is being kept on this very powerful nation, Russia, because they are right there. They are right next to—to our state.[58]

Again, Fey (with Poehler as Couric) took a light hand in making fun of Palin's long-winded answers. In an *SNL* skit that aired a few days after the Couric interview, she kept the message closely linked to the original, adding a few comedic touches:

Poehler, as Couric: On foreign policy, I want to give you one more chance to explain your claim that you have foreign policy experience based on Alaska's proximity to Russia. What did you mean by that?

Fey, as Palin: Well, Alaska and Russia are only separated by a narrow maritime border. You got Alaska here, this right here is water, and this is Russia. So, we keep an eye on them.

Poehler: And how do you do that exactly?

Fey: Every morning, when Alaskans wake up, one of the first things they do, is look outside to see if there are any Russians hanging around. And if there are, you gotta go up to them and ask, "What are you doing here?" and if they can't give you a good reason, it's our responsibility to say, you know, "Shoo! Get back over there!"[59]

Into the National Spotlight

Americans of all political persuasions were captivated by the performances. "We all knew that Palin and Fey looked alike. But as alike as this? Height: identical. Shade of hair: identical. Size and shape of ears: identical,"[60] observed one reporter. Said fellow comedian and *SNL* star Darrell Hammond, "I've never seen a better impression. If they put those two on a sonar, they would match up electronically."[61] Indeed, with her performances as Palin, "Tina Fey" became a household name—and at times was even mistaken for the vice-presidential candidate. "It's the most ridiculous, borderline-dangerous thing that the Republican vice-presidential nominee happened to look like the funniest woman working in America," said *SNL* writer Adam McKay. "What if the next Republican presidential nominee looks exactly like [actor and comedian] Seth Rogen?"[62]

Fey's wildly popular performance catapulted her into the national spotlight. Even people who did not typically watch *SNL* or other projects she had been a part of now knew who Tina Fey was.

A Woman with Strong Morals

Tina Fey is similar to many of the characters she has created and portrayed. Like Liz Lemon, her character in *30 Rock*, Fey perseveres and is professionally driven. She has the moral authority of Ms. Norbury, the math teacher she portrayed in *Mean Girls*. In *Baby Mama*, Fey played fertility-challenged Kate Holbrook, a character who reflects Fey's own straitlaced personality. Fey has also taken on roles that have seemingly little in common with her real-life self. In *Unbreakable Kimmy Schmidt*, for instance, she appeared as Marcia, a foolish lawyer (a parody of the famous lawyer Marcia Clark), in the first season of the show and returned in its second seaon to play an alcoholic therapist named Andrea. In the film *Sisters*, Fey played an irresponsible woman who cannot seem to get her life together. These characters stand in sharp contrast to her actual hardworking, upstanding personality. Perhaps Fey's ability to make fun of herself may have helped her to take on these out-of-character roles.

Hard Work and High Standards

Fey is known as an incredibly hard worker. For example, she took only 43 days of maternity leave from *SNL* when her daughter Alice was born in 2005. At the time, she said, "I had to get back

Fey is a very driven woman who sets high standards for herself.

to work … NBC has me under contract; the baby and I only have a verbal agreement."[63] Although she was joking, clearly something drives Fey to push herself to the extreme edge, taking little time for rest or relaxation.

A typical day in the life of Fey is grueling by anyone's standards. On a normal day of shooting *30 Rock*, for example, Fey only had time to come home, play with her daughter, and put her to bed. Then she started writing, editing, or looking over other people's scripts. When the show was not shooting, she wrote 10 or 12 hours a day. On other days, she stayed up until the early hours, going over outlines or rewriting her own work. "I don't—and this is not an exaggeration—have time to put lotion on," she said of her busy schedule. "If I get enough time in the morning to go to the bathroom and brush my teeth and put on the clothes that I wore the day before, that's it. The idea of putting lotion on my legs, that's not happening."[64]

Fey tends to work on multiple projects simultaneously, which takes a toll on the writer herself and the people around her. For example, Fey went straight from finishing the first season of *30 Rock* to shooting *Baby Mama*, even though she had to get to work on writing *30 Rock's* second season of scripts. Some actors bring pets, family members, or stylists to the set of the movie they are filming, but not Fey—while on the set of *Baby Mama*, Fey brought the *30 Rock* writers with her so that they could get a jump on writing the show's second season. She took on a similarly hectic schedule when *Mean Girls* was being made.

Even when she is working on just one project at a time, Fey demands the most of herself and the people around her. It was common for her to bring writers home with her after a day at the *30 Rock* studio so that she could be with her daughter and get work done at the same time. "We continue writing until I can no longer stay awake," she said at the time. "I would be lying if I said there were not tears involved at home occasionally—just occasionally. The life of the working parent is constantly saying, 'This is impossible,' and then you just keep doing it."[65]

Fey expects the people she collaborates with to work as hard as she does. She has a reputation for having very high standards, for herself and the people around her. "Sometimes, people expect that I'm going to be tough," she said. "It's not a bad situation. People treat you better. People are on time."[66] It is well known that Fey is a bit of a perfectionist and likes to monitor the work of the people around her. Amy Poehler once said, "Tina likes to be at the top of the mountain, keeping an eye on things."[67]

Despite her tough standards and rigid expectations, Fey manages to be well liked by most people with whom she works. One reporter who followed her behind the scenes at *SNL* observed the following about her work demeanor: "Fey was considerate and accessible. She solicited a range of opinions, paid earnest compliments ... Only every now and then did she turn to a writer and say something like ' ... how long did it take you to come up with that?'"[68]

Snarky and Insecure

Although no one Fey knows describes her as a mean person, almost everyone around her recognizes that her humor can have a nasty edge to it. One reporter said, "Nearly all Fey's colleagues [at *SNL*] mentioned her ability to be mean and disarming at the same time. I heard her humor variously described as 'hard-edged,' 'vicious,' and 'cruel.'"[69] Fey does not intend to come off as cruel or unpleasant, though she does admit she possesses an extraordinary gift for coming up with sarcastic comments. "I'm not a mean person, but I have a capacity for it," she admits. "I have the biting comment formed somewhere in the back of my head—like it's in captivity."[70]

Despite her capacity for biting comments, Fey is actually a very sensitive person and even insecure at times. For example, when it was proposed that she not only write but also star in *30 Rock*, Fey at first hesitated, wondering if she was getting too old for on-camera work or if she was really the person viewers wanted to see for half an hour on their TVs. However, she realized she had to have more confidence in herself and tried to think more like the male comedians she has seen rise to success with their own shows.

Husband, Coworker, and Friend: Jeff Richmond

Fey's husband, Jeff Richmond, is also very talented. He has acted in and produced television shows, but he is best known for composing music.

Richmond went to Kent State University, where he worked on the scores of several musicals. He met Fey in Chicago, where they worked together in Second City—she as an actor and he as a musician. Shortly after Fey went to work at *SNL*, Richmond was hired there as a composer. He left *SNL* in 2006 to compose music for his wife's show, *30 Rock*, where he also appeared as an extra. He composed music for Fey's movie *Baby Mama* and was a producer for *Sisters* and *Whiskey Tango Foxtrot*. Richmond currently works alongside Fey on the set of *Unbreakable Kimmy Schmidt*, for which he

Fey married Jeff Richmond in 2001.

is the composer and a producer. Of their working relationship, Fey said: "We're not literally together all day. That would make anybody crazy. But it's a good situation because we work toward the same goal ... Last year, he did have an issue with a particular story for the show. He was like, 'Listen, I'm going to tell you something because nobody tells you no—I don't like this.'"[1]

Reporters have often commented on the comfortable relationship enjoyed by Fey and Richmond. Perhaps this is because they dated for seven years before marrying on June 3, 2001. When together, they tend to act and speak with the relaxed intimacy of people who have known each other for a very long time. Even though he is 10 years older than her, they seem to be very good friends with a lot in common. Their favorite pastimes revolve around spending time with their daughters, Alice (born September 10, 2005) and Penelope (born August 10, 2011).

Fey is shown here with her daughter Penelope in 2012.

1. Quoted in Oprah Winfrey, "Oprah Talks to Tina Fey," *O, The Oprah Magazine*, February 2009. www.oprah.com/omagazine/oprah-winfrey-interviews-tina-fey#ixzz4RvIf2t93.

Cannot Take a Compliment

Even though the rest of the world has embraced her as an intelligent, attractive celebrity, Fey continues to make self-deprecating jokes and put herself down when complimented by others. For example, when *People* magazine called to tell her they had nominated her as one of the 50 Most Beautiful People of 2003, her first response was to take a shot at herself. She told the person who was calling, "I've been reading the '50 Most Beautiful People' issue for years, and there's always one person on the list who makes you think, 'Give me a ... break.' This year, I'm proud to be that person."[71]

Likewise, when one interviewer asked if she would be happier trading her hectic, work-heavy lifestyle for a day at the beach with a pack of photographers snapping illicit shots of her bikini-clad body, she sarcastically replied, "Boy, that'd be bad for all parties because that thing is gone."[72] Like many people who have undergone a dramatic physical transformation, Fey has trouble seeing herself as anything other than the awkward girl she was in high school. "Tina has remained self-deprecating, even as she has glammed up," said friend and *30 Rock* cowriter Kay Cannon. "She'll always see herself as that other, the thing she came from."[73]

A "Good Girl"

Fey's sense of morality was well established by the time she was in high school, when she reserved her meanest jokes and nicknames for the kids who drank, took drugs, cut class, and dressed inappropriately. She thinks smoking is disgusting, and she has never touched drugs. Unlike Andrea, the oft-drunk therapist she played in the second season of *Unbreakable Kimmy Schmidt*, Fey rarely drinks alcohol.

As an adult, Fey continues to judge others for what she considers inappropriate behavior. She openly disapproves of rude people and will reportedly say something if she sees a

Sticking to Principles

Fey holds a special dislike for people who cheat. According to her husband, Fey regards cheating as one of the worst things a person can do. She regards being in a relationship as signing up to agree to certain rules—and she has no tolerance for those who break them. If someone is married, she also thinks it is wrong for them to flirt with anyone who is not their spouse. "She has her principles, and she sticks to her principles more than anybody I've ever met in my life," her husband said. "She's very black-and-white."[1]

1. Quoted in Maureen Dowd, "What Tina Wants," *Vanity Fair*, January 2009. www.vanityfair.com/magazine/2009/01/tina_fey200901?currentPage=1.

person spit on the sidewalk or have too much to drink. She dislikes people who cut in line or otherwise cheat others to get what they want. "She's pretty monastic at times,"[74] said Poehler, meaning that Fey's behavior can resemble that of a monk. Richmond, Fey's husband, agrees: "I don't know if she's judgmental—maybe 'fascinated.' Nah, 'judgmental' is the right word [to describe her]."[75]

Fey attributes her reserved character to growing up in the 1980s under the influence of Nancy Reagan's "Just Say No" antidrug campaign. Fey said she took Reagan's instructions literally—and just said no to everything. "I don't enjoy any kind of danger or volatility," she said. "I don't have that kind of 'I love the bad guys' thing. No, no thank you. I like nice people."[76] Fey exudes this "good-girl" persona in her home life and hobbies, too. She is very soft-spoken and likes to sew and bake cookies. A satisfying night for her might include indulging in some cupcakes (her favorite dessert) or maybe a big hunk of cheese. Perhaps as a result of her own personal physical transformation, she loves to watch television shows

Charity Work

Throughout her career, Fey has participated in many events for charity. Much of her charitable work is for organizations that focus on helping women and children achieve stability and success in their daily lives. Fey also supports gender equality in the entertainment industry.

Fey's charity work often supports the welfare of children around the world. She and her husband, Jeff Richmond, participated in the 2012 benefit concert for the Children's Health Fund, a group that aims to provide health services to children in need across the United States. In 2013, Fey and Poehler held a Golden Globes after-party to benefit Worldwide Orphans.

Fey also supports groups such as Autism Speaks, Stand Up to Cancer, and Love Our Children, which fights violence against children. In 2015, Fey was one of several celebrities to take the stage at the 2nd Annual LOL with LLS, a comedy night benefitting the Leukemia & Lymphoma Society. The event took place on May 18, 2015, which was Fey's 45th birthday.

that deal with renovation, such as cosmetic makeovers and home improvement.

When asked by *New York Times* columnist Maureen Dowd what the wildest thing she has ever done is, Fey replied, "Nothing."[77] Fey projects a strict morality onto her projects, too. For example, in *Baby Mama*, when her character, Kate, is persuaded to go out clubbing, she innocently agrees, saying, "[Well,] there is a new ginger body splash I've been dying to try."[78] Likewise, the character she wrote and played in *Mean Girls*, Ms. Norbury, is, as Fey puts it, "the moral compass of the movie."[79] As Fey would like to do in real life, Ms. Norbury helps the movie's mean girls come to terms with their insecurities and encourages them to feel good about themselves, rather than

Fey is shown here with fellow comedian Nick Kroll at a Leukemia & Lymphona Society benefit in 2015.

degrade themselves by dumbing themselves down for boys. In countless other scenarios, Fey's devotion to a strict understanding of right and wrong is evident.

Seeking More Positive Portrayals

Fey is disheartened by the long history of unrealistic beauty standards in society. For example, Fey thinks facelifts and other plastic surgery modifications make women look unoriginal. She feels that celebrities in the 1960s and 1970s "weren't as homogenized as they are today. [N]ow they're all so fake-looking, and the same kind of fake-looking."[80] In her 2011 book, *Bossypants*, she wrote, "'Why can't we accept the human form as it is?' screams no one. I don't know why, but we never have. That's why people wore corsets and neck stretchers and powdered wigs."[81]

Fey tries to keep her looks low-key. Being real and not hiding behind clothes and makeup is important to her, and she tries to instill the same values in her daughters. Fey said, "Sometimes, I like to watch those *Real Housewives* TV shows, and Alice will be there and I'll say, 'See how these ladies have put all this goop in their face, isn't that funny? That's silly, right? Why would they do that?' And that is hopefully going to be the thing that keeps me from doing it."[82]

As for pictures taken of her, Fey will allow some airbrushing and touch-ups. "The most I've changed pictures out of vanity was to edit around any shot where you can see my butt," she said. "I like to look goofy," she explained, "but I also don't want to get canceled because of my big old butt."[83] Although Fey would never consider plastic surgery or Botox, she thinks digitally adjusting certain unflattering pictures of herself is a fair compromise.

Against Objectifying Women

Fey is strongly against the objectification of women. She has been particularly hostile toward the *Girls Gone Wild* franchise, which broadcasts the drunken antics of college-aged girls. "Ladies, don't show [yourselves] to [*Girls Gone Wild* creator] Joe Francis. Get your own camera, film [yourselves], and get the money,"[84] she said. Although Fey is partly joking, she is sincere in her dislike of men whom she has said take advantage of women. For this reason, she always advises women to take charge of their own lives.

Not surprisingly, Fey also hates clubs that feature naked or barely-clothed women. She considers them to be disrespect-ful—both to the women on the stage and to the wives and girlfriends of the men who visit them. "I feel like we all need to be better than that," she said. "That industry needs to die, by all of us being a little bit better than that."[85]

Interestingly, however, Fey has written and acted in many scenes that take place at these kinds of clubs. For example, the pilot episode of *30 Rock* shows Fey's character Liz Lemon going to one of these clubs, drinking, and getting onstage to dance. In another example, from a third-season episode of *30 Rock*, Lemon is forced to go to one of these clubs with her staff. As if to remind both her staff and the audience of what these places are really all about, she says with fake excitement, "Let's go see some naked daughters and moms!"[86]

Fey is not only concerned with young women getting unhealthy messages about sexuality and womanhood; she is also concerned about even younger girls, such as her daughter, Alice. As a two-year-old, Alice liked to play with princess figurines. "I think this is ingenious marketing, but that princess thing sets off an alarm bell for me," Fey said. She added that she is bothered by the qualities of helplessness or defenselessness she feels some fictional princesses represent and is especially upset by the lengths that some classic female animated characters went to in order to attract men. For example, she is disturbed by the idea "that a girl would really aspire to be the Little Mermaid, a beautiful redhead with no legs who waits for her prince! Who literally gives up her voice! What are we doing? What's going on?"[87]

Dealing with Her Fears

At times, Fey can be an intensely fearful person, which probably stems from the slashing attack she suffered as a five-year-old. For example, although all Americans were frightened and haunted by the terrorist attacks of September 11, 2001, Fey was traumatized by them and even considered moving away from New York City as a result.

Fey was also deeply upset later that year, when the deadly

Meeting Ms. Palin

After weeks of enduring Fey's merciless imperson-ations of her, Sarah Palin made arrangements to appear on *Saturday Night Live*. Fey agonized over meeting Palin. She reportedly told friend Conan O'Brien (host of the late-night talk show *Conan*) that even though she knew it was her job to make fun of Palin, she was nervous about doing it to her face because Palin was first and foremost a human being and a mom.

That is why Fey arranged a skit that minimized the amount of mocking she would have to do of Palin. The sketch featured the real and fake Palins walking silently past each other, looking each other up and down—and that is where the interaction ended. Fey said she wanted to minimize the amount of time they were on-screen together in part because it would be too uncomfortable to make fun of Palin in person.

toxin anthrax was anonymously sent to the building where *Saturday Night Live* is filmed. Anthrax is a very serious and potentially deadly disease caused by exposure to a bacterium called *Bacillus anthracis*. She recalled sitting in her dressing room on a Friday, writing copy for that week's "Weekend Update," when she heard on the news that anthrax had been discovered at 30 Rockefeller Plaza, the address of the studios. Without a word to anyone, Fey immediately left the building, hurrying past guest stars, and headed straight for her house, crying the whole way home.

Although all the people in the building were evacuated, everyone came back—except Fey. She was indescribably struck with fear and was convinced everyone in the build-ing was going to die. She was so shaken up, in fact, that she needed therapy to cope with the event. After talking to a thera-pist, Fey recognized the connection between her reaction to

Fey loves being with her family. She is shown here at a baseball game with them in 2012.

the anthrax incident and the attack she suffered as a little girl. "It's the attack out of nowhere," she said. "Something comes out of nowhere, it's horrifying,"[88] she said.

Even though much of her career has involved making light of sensational news events, Fey prefers a quieter, calmer world. "I want every day to be the most boring news day ever," she said. "I want every day to be about spelling bee champions and baby basketball. It's better to have no comedy material than a horrific news day."[89] In fact, when she describes her ideal day, it is not very glamorous at all: She and her husband take their daughters to a playground at a nearby park and then go to a restaurant around the corner from their house for burgers, fries, and milkshakes.

Chapter **Five**

Facing the Future

Tina Fey's career hit a new high in 2008, thanks in part to the success of her film projects and television series *30 Rock*, and her popular portrayal of governor Sarah Palin on *SNL*. Fey continues to write and star in various film and television productions, including the wildly popular *Unbreakable Kimmy Schmidt*, which was picked up by the television streaming service Netflix in 2014. Fey continues to stand out among her peers as a dynamic talent.

Affecting the Election

It was the Palin performances that launched Fey into superstardom in 2008. To this day, people are still discussing to what extent her sketches may have influenced the outcome of the 2008 presidential election.

Although it cannot be known to what extent the public was affected by the performances, or whether they were influenced positively or negatively, surveys show that Americans were impacted. According to one poll conducted by the Pew Research Center in October 2008, the American public was slightly more familiar with Fey's *Saturday Night Live* version of Palin than with the real Palin. For example, 42 percent said they had either seen or heard about Fey's portrayal of Palin on *SNL*, while 41 percent said that they had either seen or heard about Palin's real interview with Katie Couric. Furthermore, after Fey's spoof of Palin's interview with Couric, awareness of and interest in the real interviews increased. Americans were also much more aware of Fey's sketches than they were of Republican presidential nominee John McCain's campaign appearances made during the same time (only 34 percent said they were aware of these).

Some analysts, such as Lauren Feldman, a communications professor at American University, believed the hype surrounding Fey's performances altered the outcome of the election by cementing negative views about Palin in the public's mind. "The more you see Tina Fey sending up Sarah Palin's style of speech, her folksy mannerisms, and her lack of knowledge," Feldman said, "the more those characteristics rise to the top of your mind when you come to listen to the real Sarah Palin, and that influences your assessment of her."[90] As one reporter writing for the *New York Times* put it, "It could be that the McCain campaign has concluded that what Palin really faces is a Tina Fey problem: Fey's impersonation of Palin has proved so dead-on—and popular—that it has further undermined Palin's plausibility."[91]

Palin Shines on SNL

On October 18, 2008, in a much-anticipated broadcast, Palin guest-starred on *SNL*, coming face-to-face with Fey-as-Palin. Audiences were mesmerized as Palin and Fey walked silently past each other, as identical as mirror images. During the broadcast, Palin allowed herself to be mocked as "Caribou Barbie" and danced along to a rap about her

A Boost in Popularity

Fey's appearances as Palin heightened her profile—a New York marketing firm estimated that the sketch performances made Fey recognizable to 6 out of every 10 Americans. They also helped *SNL* enjoy a surge in popularity. More than 10 million people tuned in to watch the first Fey-as-Palin sketch in September 2008. *SNL* had not enjoyed an audience of that size since 2001, when people tuned in after the September 11th attacks to see how the distinctly New York show would handle humor in the aftermath of the crisis.

By Fey's second appearance as Palin, the number of viewers topped 17 million, and even more people tuned in online. In all, the 5 sketches featuring Fey as Palin generated more than 27 million views on NBC.com, and more than 68 million views on video-sharing websites such as YouTube. During the show on which Palin herself appeared, *SNL* experienced its highest ratings since 1994.

For the second time in her career, it appeared that Fey helped revive *SNL* as a relevant show. Overall, the "Feylin" performances helped boost *SNL*'s ratings by more than 76 percent over the previous year's ratings.

and her husband that mocked their Alaskan lifestyle. "Just two weeks before the election," wrote one *New York Times* reporter, "the Republicans are not pulling out all the stops to frame Palin as a knowledgeable, thoughtful vice president; they are showcasing her as a star."[92]

Not everyone thought that Palin's appearance on the show helped her, though. In fact, the next day, former Secretary of State Colin Powell chose to endorse Barack Obama, even though Powell had served in the Republican administration of George W. Bush and was expected to endorse the Republican ticket.

A Change of Heart

Palin herself seemed comfortable with the portrayals of her, saying she thought Fey looked a lot like her and that she had been a longtime fan of the actress. She watched the first sketch from her plane and reportedly laughed out loud.

After she lost the election, however, her opinion about Fey's spoofs apparently changed. In a conservative documentary, Palin claimed that Fey spent the election season capitalizing on and even exploiting the public's interest in her. "I did see that Tina Fey was named

Fey reprised her role as Sarah Palin on *Saturday Night Live* during the 2016 election season.

entertainer of the year ... that's a little bit perplexing, but it also says a great deal about our society,"[93] said Palin. Fey said she has no remorse about the sketches. "I feel clean about it," she said. "All those jokes were fair hits."[94]

Fey never wanted the sketches to last more than a few weeks. Just before the election, she said: "If she wins, I'm done. I can't do that for four years. And by 'I'm done,' I mean I'm leaving Earth."[95] When McCain and Palin lost the election, the demands of Fey's already intense workload and her fear of being typecast into one role led her to feel relieved that she no longer had to play the politician with any kind of regularity. Fey returned to *SNL* to impersonate Palin in 2010 and 2011. In early 2016, she brought the character back again to spoof Palin's endorsement of Republican Donald Trump as a presidential candidate.

Award After Award

Fey's success as Palin was coupled with an astounding number of awards won by *30 Rock*. Although at first it was slow to gain viewership, *30 Rock* ultimately won major industry awards in several categories, showing that critics and viewers alike thought it was one of the best shows on television.

Many of the actors on the show won awards for their performances, with Fey winning the Screen Actors Guild Award for Outstanding Performance by a Female Actor in a Comedy Series in 2008, 2009, and 2012. The show also won the Writers Guild of America Award for Best Comedy Series in 2008 and 2009. Another honor *30 Rock* won was the Producers Guild of America's Danny Thomas Award for Outstanding Producer of Episodic Television, Comedy from 2008 to 2010. In addition, the show won the Outstanding Achievement in Comedy Award from the Television Critics Association and a Peabody Award in 2008, along with several Golden Globe Awards.

For its second season, *30 Rock* broke records when

Fey has become a familiar face on red carpets at award shows because of her success as an actress, writer, and producer.

Shown here is the cast of *30 Rock* at the 61st Primetime Emmy Awards in 2009, where they won an award for Outstanding Comedy Series.

it received 17 Emmy nominations, making it the most-nominated comedy series for any individual year at the time. In 2009, *30 Rock* again broke records when its third season was nominated for 22 Emmy awards. Over the course of the show's 7 seasons, *30 Rock* won 16 of the 103 Emmy Awards that it was nominated for. Fey has won several individual awards for writing specific episodes and for her acting in the series. The final episode of *30 Rock* aired in 2013.

A Relatable and Loveable Woman

Liz Lemon, Fey's character on *30 Rock*, resonated with viewers. They connected to her realistic, career-woman lifestyle and the challenges that came along with it. One writer described Lemon as "arguably the most realistic single career woman to appear on TV since Mary Tyler Moore."[96]

Indeed, Lemon's career-driven, chronically single,

food-obsessed lifestyle has resonated with many women. For example, Lemon prefers a perfect sandwich to a perfect man; her ideal night is to curl up in comfortable clothes after a long day at work with a big plate of cheese. Similar to Kate Holbrook (Fey's character in *Baby Mama*), who opted for promotions rather than parenthood throughout her 20s and 30s, Lemon—like many women—sacrificed her personal

A Sexist Portrayal?

One complaint about Fey's impression of Palin was that it was sexist. In September 2008, McCain campaign adviser Carly Fiorina came out against the sketch in which Fey imitated Palin while Poehler imitated Hillary Clinton. "The portrait was very dismissive of the substance of Sarah Palin," Fiorina complained. "They were defining Hillary Clinton as very substantive and Sarah Palin as totally superficial. I think that continues the line of argument that is disrespectful in the extreme, and yes, I would say, sexist."[1]

Fey rejected the accusation that her portrayals of Palin were sexist. If anything, she thought the accusations themselves were sexist because they painted Palin as a woman who was unable to take a joke in the same way a man would. "The implication was that she's so fragile, which she is not. She's a strong woman," Fey said. "Also, [these accusations are] sexist because, like, who would ever go on the news and say, 'That seemed awful mean to George Bush when [actor] Will Ferrell [played him].'"[2] Fey maintains that all the jokes she wrote about Palin were fair and in the spirit of fun.

1. Quoted in Access Hollywood, "McCain Camp Calls Fey's Palin Portrayal 'Sexist,'" Today.com, September 16, 2008. www.msnbc.msn.com/id/26743182.

2. Quoted in Maureen Dowd, "What Tina Wants," *Vanity Fair*, January 2009. www.vanityfair.com/magazine/2009/01/tina_fey200901?currentPage=1.

life for professional success. In doing so, she had to contend with overbearing male colleagues to whom society has been much kinder.

It is for all of these reasons that millions tuned in each week to hear observations such as, "No one has it harder in this country today than women," as Lemon says in one episode of *30 Rock*. "It turns out we can't be president. We can't be network news anchors. Madonna's arms look crazy."[97] Lemon's sympathy for the physical, professional, and personal stresses put upon America's women is at the heart of what makes her so relatable and lovable.

Not Slowing Down

With no plans to slow down, Fey charged ahead with a full schedule. On top of continuing her work with *30 Rock*, Fey did voiceover work for the Japanese animated film *Ponyo*, which was released in 2009. She had another voiceover part in 2010's animated film *Megamind* with comedian Will Ferrell. She also narrated the Disneynature documentary *Monkey Kingdom*, which was released in 2015.

When she was not in the studio recording voiceovers, Fey was either in front of or behind the camera, as well as on the red carpet. In 2013, Fey was invited to host the 70th Annual Golden Globe Awards with longtime friend Amy Poehler. Fey and Poehler had a three-year contract with the awards ceremony, and the duo returned to host again in 2014 and 2015 for the 71st and 72nd Golden Globes, respectively.

Fey worked on the movie *The Invention of Lying*, which starred many big names, including Ricky Gervais, Jennifer Garner, Louis C. K., Rob Lowe, and Jonah Hill. The greatly anticipated film was released in September 2009. Fey also began working on another movie called *Date Night*. She starred alongside Steve Carell, also a former member of Second City. The film was released in 2010. In addition, Fey filmed a series of American Express television commercials.

After *30 Rock* ended in 2013, Fey took on several new acting projects. She starred in a romantic comedy-drama called *Admission* with Paul Rudd, which was released in 2013. The next year, Fey starred alongside Jason Bateman in *This Is Where I Leave You*, based on a book of the same name by Jonathan Tropper. Critics and audiences generally did not respond well to either film.

Fey also made a cameo appearance in *Anchorman 2: The Legend Continues*, which was released in 2013, and she rounded out 2014 with an appearance in the film *Muppets Most Wanted*. In 2015, Fey starred in the comedy *Sisters* with Poehler, and in 2016, she starred in *Whiskey Tango Foxtrot*, a film based on Kim Baker's memoir *The Taliban Shuffle: Strange Days in Afghanistan and Pakistan*. Both *Sisters* and *Whiskey Tango Foxtrot* were met with mixed reviews.

A New Book and a New Baby

Juggling multiple projects is second nature to Fey. In 2008, she signed a major book deal with Little, Brown Book Group. According to the *New York Observer*, the deal was worth $6 million. Fey's contract reportedly stated that part of the proceeds would go toward building six libraries for schoolchildren in underserved New York neighborhoods and that a gift would be made to Books for Kids, a nonprofit foundation promoting literacy. Fey's book, a humorous autobiography titled *Bossypants*, was published in 2011. It spent five weeks on the New York Times Best Sellers list. Fey was nominated for a Grammy Award in 2012 for Best Spoken Word Album for her recorded reading of *Bossypants*.

In 2011, while promoting her book on *The Oprah Winfrey Show*, Fey announced that she was pregnant with her second child. Fey and husband Jeff Richmond welcomed their daughter Penelope into the world on August 10, 2011. Fey took a break from her work on *30 Rock* to spend time with her new baby. In regards to being a working mother, Fey had

Bossypants was another successful project for Fey.

some insightful words in *Bossypants*. "The biggest thing you realize when you have a kid," she wrote, "is how many other people in your workplace are dealing with that ... It makes you more of a sympathetic human being."[98]

Unbreakable *Tina Fey*

Fey has had a good run with movie and book projects, but her biggest successes are in television, perhaps because this is where her heart truly is. "My logical brain plan would be to do more writing for movies because it's a friendlier family lifestyle," Fey once commented during an interview. "But I don't know if I'd be able to stop myself from trying to do TV again."[99]

Fey is seen here with the stars of *Unbreakable Kimmy Schmidt*— Tituss Burgess, Ellie Kemper, and Carol Kane. The show has become a hit with critics and audiences.

Fey is shown here at the *Whiskey Tango Foxtrot* premiere in 2016.

Fey struck television gold again in 2015, when she created the show *Unbreakable Kimmy Schmidt* with Robert Carlock, whom she had worked with on *30 Rock*. Fey also serves as a writer and producer for the show, and she has made several on-screen appearances in various roles.

Unbreakable Kimmy Schmidt was originally produced for NBC, but it was sold to Netflix before it aired. The show quickly became a fan favorite, and Netflix immediately renewed it for a second season. *Unbreakable Kimmy Schmidt* also has been well-received by critics and was nominated for multiple Primetime Emmy Awards in 2015 and 2016. Some have found the series to be offensive, but Fey has taken a stand against explaining its jokes. "We did an *Unbreakable Kimmy Schmidt* episode and the Internet was in a whirlwind, calling it 'racist,' but my new goal is not to explain jokes," Fey said in an interview with Net-A-Porter's magazine *The Edit*. "I feel like we put so much effort into writing and crafting everything, they need to speak for themselves. There's a real culture of demanding apologies, and I'm opting out of that."[100] In January 2016, Netflix announced that *Unbreakable Kimmy Schmidt* would return for a third season.

Flying Under Hollywood's Radar

Fey is one of the most sought-after women in show business, but fame has not made her any less caring, modest, or hardworking. Close friends say she is still the type to call before coming over and to pick up coffee for office assistants if she is getting any for herself. When recognized in public, she gets shy, embarrassed, and even awkward. "This woman came up to me," she said of an encounter with a fan in an electronics store. "She was like, 'You're a great actress.' And I was like, 'Oh, I don't think so, but thank you.' And she said, 'No, I'm asking you, you're an actress, right?' I said, 'Oh, don't worry about it.' All I could think of to say was, 'Don't worry about it.'"[101] Perhaps it is because she spent so many years behind the writer's desk instead of in front of the camera that Fey still has trouble thinking of herself as a famous actress who is likely to be recognized in public.

Fey fears great fame will interfere with her ability to do the kind of work she really wants to do. She worries that becoming too big will cause her to get caught up in worrying about ratings, advertisers, public relations, paparazzi, and other markers of megastardom that could interfere with her true goals: working hard and making entertaining movies and television shows. "They should draw up an equation: What level of fame do you need to achieve to keep doing what you want? Because you don't want any more than that," she said. Ideally, Fey would like to remain just slightly under Hollywood's radar so that she can continue to live her life and do her work. "How do you get to ... just live your life, make hilarious movies with your friends, and then go home,"[102] she wonders, and she hopes to achieve this kind of balance in her life.

Planning for Her Future

Fey aims to keep working as hard as she can while she is still on top of the entertainment industry. At the moment, studios and production companies cover many of Fey's expenses, but she anticipates a day when she will have to pay for travel and other expenses herself. She also hopes that she realizes when her career is over and that she will not resort to appearing on reality TV shows out of desperation to remain relevant. She wants to continue to make "smart" comedy and not "fall into the trap of just cranking out things that are good enough to sell."[103]

What is next for Tina Fey? As of 2016, she has a new comedy series in the works for NBC, with Fey, Robert Carlock (*Unbreakable Kimmy Schmidt*), and Tracey Wigfield (*30 Rock* and *The Mindy Project*) teaming up as producers. The

Tina Fey is ready for whatever the future holds.

13-episode series, tentatively titled *Great News*, is set to premiere in 2017. NBC hopes the show will bring new life to its deflated comedic lineup. With Fey, Carlock, and Wigfield—a trio of comedy geniuses—at the wheel, there is a good chance that *Great News* will be a great success.

Notes

Introduction: A Newsworthy Comedian

1. Quoted in Ed Pilkington, "Tina Fey for Vice President!" *Sydney Morning Herald* (Australia), October 23, 2008. www.smh.com.au/news/lifeandstyle/people/tina-fey-for-vicepresident/2008/10/22/1224351411852.html.

2. Quoted in MSNBC, "Tina Fey 'Leaving Earth' If Palin Wins," Today.com, October 13, 2008. www.today.com/id/27164270/ns/today-today_entertainment/t/tina-fey-leaving-earth-if-palin-wins/#.WEmCQaIrJBw.

3. Quoted in Kristen Baldwin, "Tina Fey: One Hot 'Mama,'" *Entertainment Weekly*, April 9, 2008. www.ew.com/article/2008/04/10/tina-fey-one-hot-mama.

Chapter One: A Funny Upbringing

4. Quoted in Maureen Dowd, "What Tina Wants," *Vanity Fair*, January 2009. www.vanityfair.com/culture/2009/01/tina-fey200901.

5. Quoted in Virginia Heffernan, "Anchor Woman: Tina Fey Rewrites Late-Night Comedy," *The New Yorker*, November 3, 2003. www.newyorker.com/magazine/2003/11/03/anchor-woman.

6. Quoted in David Hiltbrand, "A 'Grounded' Tina Fey Expands Her Territory to Movies," *Philadelphia Inquirer*, April 28, 2004. www.elon.edu/e-web/pendulum/Issues/2004/5_6/onlinefeatures/tina.xhtml.

7. Quoted in Noel Murray, "Tina Fey," A.V. Club, November 1, 2006. www.avclub.com/articles/tina-fey,14025.

8. Quoted in Dowd, "What Tina Wants."

9. Quoted in Dowd, "What Tina Wants."

10. Quoted in Dowd, "What Tina Wants."

11. Brett Baer and Dave Finkel, "Fireworks," *30 Rock*, season 1, episode 18, directed by Beth McCarthy, aired April 5, 2007.

12. Quoted in Eric Spitznagel, "Tina Fey," *Believer*, November 2003. www.believermag.com/issues/200311/?read=interview_fey.

13. Quoted in Fox News, "Tina Fey Gets the Last Laugh," April 25, 2004. www.foxnews.com/story/2004/04/25/tina-fey-gets-last-laugh.html.

14. Quoted in Fox News, "Tina Fey Gets the Last Laugh."

15. Quoted in Spitznagel, "Tina Fey."

16. Quoted in George Everit, "Tina Fey," SuicideGirls.com, April 27, 2004. www.suicidegirls.com/interviews/Tina+Fey.

17. Quoted in Hiltbrand, "A 'Grounded' Tina Fey Expands Her Territory to Movies."

18. Quoted in Heffernan, "Anchor Woman."

19. Quoted in Murray, "Tina Fey."

20. Quoted in Spitznagel, "Tina Fey."

21. Quoted in Heffernan, "Anchor Woman."

22. Quoted in Heffernan, "Anchor Woman."

23. Quoted in Spitznagel, "Tina Fey."

24. Quoted in Spitznagel, "Tina Fey."

Chapter Two: Tina Fey Takes New York

25. Quoted in Heffernan, "Anchor Woman."

26. Quoted in Kelly Tracy, "Funny Girl," *CosmoGirl*, February 2008.

27. Quoted in Heffernan, "Anchor Woman."

28. Quoted in Heffernan, "Anchor Woman."

29. Quoted in Emily Rems, "Mrs. Saturday Night," *Bust*, Spring 2004, p. 42.

30. Quoted in Rems, "Mrs. Saturday Night."

31. Quoted in Rems, "Mrs. Saturday Night."

32. Quoted in Dowd, "What Tina Wants."

33. Quoted in Dowd, "What Tina Wants."

34. Quoted in Dowd, "What Tina Wants."

35. Quoted in Dowd, "What Tina Wants."

36. Quoted in Caroline Ryder, "A Conversation with *30 Rock*'s Tina Fey," *Women's Health*, January 25, 2007. www.womenshealthmag.com/life/tina-fey-interview.

37. Quoted in Ashley Mateo, "Tina Fey Talks Exercise, Indulgences and Taking Risks," *Self*, June 18, 2011. www.self.com/gallery/tina-fey-slideshow.

38. Quoted in Ryder, "A Conversation with *30 Rock*'s Tina Fey."

39. Quoted in Dowd, "What Tina Wants."

40. Quoted in Dowd, "What Tina Wants."

41. Quoted in Spitznagel, "Tina Fey."

Chapter Three: Writing Her Way to Fame

42. Quoted in Jeff Otto, "IGN Interviews Tina Fey," *IGN Movies*, April 23, 2004. www.ign.com/articles/2004/04/23/ign-interviews-tina-fey.

43. *Mean Girls*, directed by Mark Waters, (2004; Paramount Pictures), DVD.

44. Quoted in Otto, "IGN Interviews Tina Fey."

45. *Mean Girls*, directed by Mark Waters.

46. Quoted in Robert K. Elder, "Movie Review: 'Mean Girls,'" *Chicago Tribune*, April 30, 2004. articles.chicagotribune.com/2004-04-30/entertainment/0404300366_1_cady-heron-plastics-cliques.

47. Quoted in Roger Ebert, "Mean Girls," *Chicago Sun-Times*, April 30, 2004. www.rogerebert.com/reviews/mean-girls-2004

48. Quoted in Paul Brownfield, "Tina Fey and Amy Poehler Gamble with the Gal-Pal Comedy 'Baby Mama,'" *Los Angeles Times*, April 20, 2008. articles.latimes.com/2008/apr/20/entertainment/ca-feypoehler20.

49. Quoted in Baldwin, "Tina Fey."

50. Quoted in Manohla Dargis, "Learning on the Job About Birthing Babies," *New York Times*, April 25, 2008. www.nytimes.com/2008/04/25/movies/25baby.html

51. Quoted in Stephanie Zacharek, "Baby Mama," Salon.com, April 23, 2008. www.salon.com/2008/04/23/baby_mama.

52. Quoted in Claudia Puig, "'Baby Mama' Brings Funny to Full Term," *USA Today*, April 26, 2008. abcnews.go.com/Entertainment/MothersDay/story?id=4728020&page=1.

53. Quoted in Wesley Morris, "A Bundle of Laughs from Two Funny Women," *Boston Globe*, April 25, 2008. www.boston.com/moviesdisplay?display=movie&id=10726.

54. Quoted in Menachem Rosensaft, "We Can't Vote for Sarah Palin If We Can't Understand What She Says," *Huffington Post*, November 1, 2008. www.huffingtonpost.com/menachem-rosensaft/we-cant-vote-for-sarah-pa_b_131015.html.

55. Quoted in Pilkington, "Tina Fey for Vice President!"

56. "CBS Evening News: Katie Couric Interviews Sarah Palin," NBC video, 6:40, from a performance aired on September 27, 2008. www.nbc.com/saturday-night-live/video/couric--palin-open/n12311?snl=1.

57. "Sarah Palin and Hillary Clinton Address the Nation," NBC video, 5:33, from a performance aired on September 13, 2008. www.nbc.com/saturday-night-live/video/sarah-palin-and-hillary-clinton-address-the-nation/n12287?snl=1.

58. Quoted in CBS News, "Palin on Foreign Policy," September 18, 2008. www.cbsnews.com/stories/2008/09/25/eveningnews/main4479062.shtml?tag=related;wc448138.

59. "CBS Evening News: Katie Couric Interviews Sarah Palin," NBC video.

60. Quoted in Pilkington, "Tina Fey for Vice President!"

61. Quoted in Dowd, "What Tina Wants."

62. Quoted in Dowd, "What Tina Wants."

Chapter Four: A Woman with Strong Morals

63. Quoted in Sarah Hall, "Tina Fey Back on 'Update,'" *E! News*, October 20, 2005. www.eonline.com/news/50931/tina-fey-back-on-update.

64. Quoted in Karen Heller, "Down-to-Earth Mother," *Philadelphia Inquirer*, April 20, 2008. www.newspapers.com/newspage/201090303/.

65. Quoted in Stephen M. Silverman, "Tina Fey: My Generation's Been Duped," *People*, March 6, 2008. people.com/celebrity/tina-fey-my-generations-been-duped.

66. Quoted in Jancee Dunn, "Tina Fey: Funny Girl," *Reader's Digest*, April 2008. www.rd.com/family/tina-fey-interview.

67. Quoted in Heffernan, "Anchor Woman."

68. Quoted in Heffernan, "Anchor Woman."

69. Quoted in Heffernan, "Anchor Woman."

70. Quoted in Dunn, "Tina Fey."

71. Quoted in Spitznagel, "Tina Fey."

72. Quoted in Baldwin, "Tina Fey."

73. Quoted in Dowd, "What Tina Wants."

74. Quoted in Heffernan, "Anchor Woman."

75. Quoted in Heffernan, "Anchor Woman."

76. Quoted in Dowd, "What Tina Wants."

77. Quoted in Dowd, "What Tina Wants."

78. *Baby Mama*, directed by Michael McCullers (2008; Universal Pictures Home Entertainment), DVD.

79. Quoted in Hiltbrand, "A 'Grounded' Tina Fey Expands Her Territory to Movies."

80. Quoted in Spitznagel, "Tina Fey."

81. Tina Fey, *Bossypants*. New York, NY: Little, Brown Book Group, 2011.

82. Quoted in "She Who Dares," *The Edit*, December 18, 2015. p. 15. www.net-a-porter.com/magazine/330/15.

83. Quoted in Dowd, "What Tina Wants."

84. Quoted in Brownfield, "Tina Fey and Amy Poehler Gamble with the Gal-Pal Comedy 'Baby Mama.'"

85. Quoted in Dowd, "What Tina Wants."

86. John Riggi and Tina Fey, "The Natural Order," *30 Rock*, season 3, episode 20, directed by Scott Ellis, aired April 30, 2009.

87. Ann Murray-Yavar, "Interview: Tina Fey Talks to Parade," Xfinity, March 10, 2008. es.xfinity.com/sdmy/blogs/tv/2008/03/10/interview-tina-fey-talks-to-parade.

88. Quoted in Dowd, "What Tina Wants."

89. Quoted in Spitznagel, "Tina Fey."

Chapter Five: Facing the Future

90. Quoted in Pilkington, "Tina Fey for Vice President!"

91. Quoted in Alessandra Stanley, "On 'SNL' It's the Real Sarah Palin, Looking Like a Real Entertainer," *New York Times*, October 19, 2008. www.nytimes.com/2008/10/20/arts/television/20watch.html.

92. Quoted in Stanley, "On 'SNL' It's the Real Sarah Palin."

93. *Media Malpractice: How Obama Got Elected and Palin Was Targeted*, directed by John Ziegler (2009; Right Reel), DVD.

94. Quoted in Dowd, "What Tina Wants."

95. Quoted in MSNBC, "'Leaving Earth' If Palin Wins."

96. Quoted in Baldwin, "Tina Fey."

97. Robert Carlock, "Believe in the Stars," *30 Rock*, season 3, episode 2, directed by Don Scardino, aired November 6, 2008.

98. Quoted in "Tina Fey Pregnant: '30 Rock' Star to Have Second Child," *Huffington Post*, April 4, 2011. www.huffingtonpost.com/2011/04/06/tina-fey-pregnant_n_845921.html.

99. Quoted in Baldwin, "Tina Fey."

100. Quoted in "She Who Dares."

101. Quoted in Baldwin, "Tina Fey."

102. Quoted in Baldwin, "Tina Fey."

103. Quoted in Oprah Winfrey, "Oprah Talks to Tina Fey," *O, The Oprah Magazine*, February 2009. www.oprah.com/omagazine/oprah-winfrey-interviews-tina-fey#ixzz4RvIf2t93.

Tina Fey Year by Year

1970

Tina Fey is born on May 18 to Donald and Zenobia "Jeanne" Fey.

1975

Fey suffers an anonymous slashing incident that scars her from the corner of her mouth to her cheek on the left side of her face.

1988

Fey graduates from Upper Darby High School.

1992

Fey graduates from the University of Virginia.

1994

Fey joins Second City's touring ensemble.

1997

Fey joins *Saturday Night Live* as a writer.

1999

Fey becomes head writer on *Saturday Night Live*, the first female to do so in the show's history.

2000

Fey is put on camera as a host for "Weekend Update," reviving the segment.

2000–2004

Fey hosts "Weekend Update" with coanchor Jimmy Fallon.

2001

Fey and the writing staff at *Saturday Night Live* win a Writers Guild of America Award for the show's 25th anniversary special; on June 3, Fey marries Jeff Richmond, the musical composer on *SNL*; Fey helps *SNL* win an Emmy for outstanding writing—an award it had not received since 1989; and Fey is named one of *Entertainment Weekly*'s Entertainers of the Year.

2003

Fey is listed among *People* magazine's 50 Most Beautiful People of the Year, a feat she will repeat in 2006, 2008, and 2009, and she is credited with helping *Saturday Night Live* attract more viewers than any other late-night show on the air at the time.

2004

Fey hosts "Weekend Update" with coanchor Amy Poehler, marking the first time in the show's history that two women have anchored the segment; *Mean Girls* is released.

2005

Fey gives birth to her daughter Alice on September 10.

2006

Fey leaves *Saturday Night Live* to produce, write, and star in a new comedy series, *30 Rock*; the first episode airs on October 11.

2007

Fey is once again named one of *Entertainment Weekly*'s Entertainers of the Year; she wins a Writers Guild of America Award for her writing on *Saturday Night Live*; and *30 Rock* wins an Emmy for Outstanding Comedy Series.

2008

Fey's Sarah Palin sketches boost *SNL*'s ratings to heights it had not enjoyed since 2001 and 1994; *30 Rock* and Fey win three Emmys: one for Outstanding Comedy Series, one for Outstanding Actress in a Comedy Series, and one for Outstanding Writing for a Comedy Series; Fey wins a Golden Globe Award for Best Actress in a Television Comedy; she wins a Screen Actors Guild Award for Outstanding Performance by a Female Actor in a Comedy Series for her work on *30 Rock*; *30 Rock* wins a Writers Guild of America Award for Outstanding Comedy Series; Fey signs a $6 million book contract; and *Baby Mama* is released.

2009

Fey wins two Golden Globe Awards for *30 Rock*, one for Best Performance by an Actress in a Television Series and one for Best Television Series; wins a Producers Guild of America Award for Producer of the Year Award in Episodic Comedy; wins two Screen Actors Guild awards for her work on *30 Rock*; and wins another Writers Guild of America Award for her writing on *30 Rock*.

2010

Fey appears in *Date Night*; voices a character in the animated film *Megamind*; she appears on *Saturday Night Live* as Sarah Palin; she wins a Screen Actors Guild Award for Outstanding Female Actor in a Comedy Series for her work in *30 Rock*; *30 Rock* wins a Producers Guild of America Award for Outstanding Comedy Series; and Fey becomes the youngest recipient of the Mark Twain Prize for American Humor.

2011

Fey gives birth to daughter Penelope on August 10; hosts *SNL* for the third time and does her Palin impression; wins a Critics' Choice Television Award for Best Actress in a Comedy Series for her work on *30 Rock*; and publishes her autobiography *Bossypants*, which spends five weeks on the Best Sellers list.

2012

Fey is nominated for a Grammy Award for Best Spoken Word Album for her reading of *Bossypants* and wins a Screen Actors Guild Award for Outstanding Performance by a Female Actor in a Comedy Series for her work on *30 Rock*.

2013

Fey hosts the 70th Annual Golden Globe Awards with Poehler; wins an Emmy award for Outstanding Writing for a Comedy Series for the "Last Lunch" episode of *30 Rock*; stars in *Admission* alongside Paul Rudd; and has a cameo appearance in *Anchorman 2: The Legend Continues*.

2014

Fey hosts the 71st Annual Golden Globe Awards with Poehler; stars in the film *This Is Where I Leave You*; and appears in the film *Muppets Most Wanted*.

2015

Fey hosts the 72nd Annual Golden Globe Awards with Poehler; stars in the film *Sisters* alongside Poehler; narrates the Disneynature documentary *Monkey Kingdom*; and creates, writes, produces, and appears in the hit Netflix series *Unbreakable Kimmy Schmidt*.

2016

Fey stars in the film *Whiskey Tango Foxtrot* and appears as Palin again on *SNL*.

For More Information

Books

Becker, Ron, Nick Marx, and Matt Sienkiewicz. *Saturday Night Live and American TV*. Bloomington, IN: Indiana University Press, 2013.
This book examines the history of *Saturday Night Live* through essays on subjects including race, gender, authorship, and comedic performance, all in the shifting social and media landscape of American television.

Cooper, Carolyn Kraemer. *Sarah Palin: A Biography*. Santa Barbara, CA: Greenwood, 2011.
This biography is a good resource for anyone looking for more background on the woman Fey became famous for impersonating.

Fey, Tina. *Bossypants*. New York, NY: Reagan Arthur Books, 2013.
This autobiographical comedy book gives an inside look at Fey's youth, time on *Saturday Night Live*, role as a mother and wife, and life as a comedy star.

Goldberg, Andy. *Improv Comedy*. Venice, CA: Grebdog Publishing, 2012.
This informational book on improv comedy features a collection of classic scene setups and exercises, advice for building engaging characters, plots and funny situations for aspiring comedians, and an exclusive interview with famous actor Bryan Cranston.

Hill, Doug, and Jeff Weingrad. *Saturday Night: A Backstage History of Saturday Night Live*. San Francisco, CA: Untreed Reads, 2011.
This book offers a behind-the-scenes look of the first 10 years of *Saturday Night Live*, including the comedy sketches that were created and the scandals that arose.

Irwin, William. *30 Rock and Philosophy: We Want to Go to There*. Hoboken, NJ: John Wiley and Sons, 2010.
The philosophical connections that can be found in Tina Fey's NBC sitcom, *30 Rock*, are explored within this book.

Kaplan, Arie. *Saturday Night Live: Shaping TV Comedy and American Culture*. Minneapolis, MN: Twenty-First Century Books, 2015.
This book looks at the history of *Saturday Night Live* and how it has influenced television comedy and American culture.

Miller, James Andrew, and Tom Shales. *Live from New York: The Complete, Uncensored History of Saturday Night Live as Told by Its Stars, Writers, and Guests*. New York, NY: Back Bay Books, 2015.
The last four decades of *Saturday Night Live's* history— told by its various stars, writers, and guests—are the focus of this book.

Poehler, Amy. *Yes Please*. New York, NY: Dey Street Books, 2014.
This book includes Poehler's personal stories, chapters written by other people in her life, lists, poetry, photographs, mantras, and advice.

Websites

IMDb: Tina Fey (www.imdb.com/name/nm0275486)
Information on Tina Fey's life and credits in the entertainment field can be viewed on the Internet Movie Database (IMDb) website.

People: **Tina Fey** (www.people.com/tag/tina-fey)
Articles and videos featuring Tina Fey can be found on the *People* magazine website.

Saturday Night Live (www.nbc.com/Saturday_Night_Live)
Videos of Tina Fey can be viewed on the *Saturday Night Live* website. They include Fey playing Sarah Palin and appearing on "Weekend Update."

Second City (www.secondcity.com/people/other/tina-fey)
Videos and information on Tina Fey's time in the comedy troupe can be viewed on the Second City website.

30 Rock (www.nbc.com/30-rock)
News, merchandise, and videos from Tina Fey's hit NBC show can be found on this website.

Index

Picture Credits

Cover, pp. 57, 73 (right) Featureflash Photo Agency/ Shutterstock.com; pp. 7, 37 Helga Esteb/Shutterstock.com; p. 9 AP Photo/Jacquelyn Martin; p. 10 Patrick McMullan/ Contributor/Patrick McMullen/Getty Images; p. 12 Stephen Lovekin/Staff/Getty Images Entertainment/Getty Images; p. 14 Gregg Deguire/Contributor/Wire Images/Getty Images; p. 17 CBS Photo Archive/Contributor/CBS/Getty Images; p. 18 Sean Pavone/Shutterstock.com; p. 20 Jupiterimages/Getty Images; p. 22 Steve Heap/Shutterstock.com; pp. 24, 60 D Dipasupil/ Contributor/FilmMagic/Getty Images; p. 27 Tinseltown/ Shutterstock.com; p. 28 s_bukley/Shutterstock.com; p. 30 Jason Kempin/Staff/Getty Images Entertainment/Getty Images; p. 31 KMazur/Contributor/WireImages/Getty Images; p. 32 Bryan Bedder/Stringer/Getty Images Entertainment/Getty Images; p. 35 Jaguar PS/Shutterstock.com; p. 43 Kevin Winter/Staff/Getty Images Entertainment/Getty Images; p. 44 Paul Hawthorne/ Staff/Getty Images Entertainment/Getty Images; p. 46 Everett Collection/Shutterstock.com; p. 47 Bryan Bedder/Staff/Getty Images Entertainment/Getty Images; p. 49 Robyn Beck/Staff/ AFP/Getty Images; p. 52 Paul J. Richards/Staff/AFP/Getty Images; p. 61 Bobby Bank/Contributor/WireImage/Getty Images; p. 65 Robin Marchant/Stringer/Getty Images Entertainment; p. 69 Michael Stewart/Contributor/Getty Images Entertainment/Getty Images; p. 73 (left) Christopher Halloran/Shutterstock.com; p. 75 George Pimentel/Contributor/WireImage/Getty Images; p. 76 Dan MacMedan/Contributor/WireImage/Getty Images; p. 80 Jim Spellman/Stringer/Getty Images Entertainment/Getty Images; p. 81 Monica Schipper/Contributor/FilmMagic/Getty Images; p. 82 Neilson Barnard/Staff/Getty Images Entertainment/ Getty Images; p. 85 John Lamparski/Contributor/WireImages/ Getty Images.

About the Author

Melissa Raé Shofner earned her bachelor's degree in creative writing from SUNY Purchase College in 2009. In 2013, she completed a master's degree in publishing through Pace University. Shofner lives with her cat, Monroe, in the suburbs of Buffalo, NY. She works full-time as a writer and editor of educational children's books. Shofner is also the senior editor for Riding Light, a literary journal based in Santa Barbara, CA. In her spare time, she enjoys reading, cooking, running, and the occasional Netflix binge.